The Rider Book of Mystical Verse

The Rider Book of
Mystical Verse

Edited by J. M. Cohen

RIDER

London Melbourne Sydney Auckland Johannesburg

Rider & Company

An imprint of the Hutchinson Publishing Group

17–21 Conway Street, London W 1 P 6 J D

Hutchinson Group (Australia) Pty Ltd
30–32 Cremorne Street, Richmond South, Victoria 3121
PO Box 151, Broadway, New South Wales 2007

Hutchinson Group (N Z) Ltd
32–34 View Road, PO Box 40–086, Glenfield, Auckland 10

Hutchinson Group (S A) Pty Ltd
PO Box 337, Bergvlei 2012, South Africa

First published 1983
This selection © J. M. Cohen 1983
Preface and certain translations © J. M. Cohen 1983

Set in Bembo by Colset Pte Ltd, Singapore

Printed in Great Britain by The Anchor Press Ltd
and bound by Wm Brendon & Son Ltd,
both of Tiptree, Essex

British Library Cataloguing in Publication Data
The Rider book of mystical verse.
1. Religious poetry, English
I. Cohen, J. M.
821'.008'0382   PR1191

ISBN 0 09 151640 4   cased
        0 09 151641 2   paperback

Contents

*To the Sangha
of the Manjushri Institute
at Conishead Priory*

Preface

'Mystical: having a certain spiritual character or import, by virtue of a connexion or union with God and transcending human comprehension.' So the *Shorter Oxford English Dictionary* defines a word that evades precise definition. For the purposes of this book, the Oxford definition can be accepted, though with certain reservations. In the first place, though transcending logical comprehension, mystical truths are often more closely glimpsed by the poets than by dealers in plain prose meanings; and secondly, though the word 'spiritual' always applies, connexion with God is not inevitable. Indeed the only definition that will cover every poem here is 'poetry of spiritual apprehension'.

Most of the poems chosen for this book are written in the language of one or another of the world's great religions: Jewish, Christian, Muslim, Hindu and Buddhist, though there are a few inclusions from ancient Mexico and Peru, and certain recent European poets – I would instance Blake and Rilke – use a symbolism hardly Christian and peculiarly their own. Ways of expression are many. But the fundamental truths are one.

The book is divided into eight sections, the poems being grouped according to the nature of their insights. So, beginning with a variety of acknowledgements of the deplorable condition of man, we pass, in the second group, to poems which offer some, often agonized, hope of transcending it. The third group, 'The Inward Eye', illustrates the widening and deepening of the senses that comes with the beginnings of contemplative practice. Sections four and five are devoted to prayer and contemplation, and to the joy and gratitude that accompanies the first contacts with the power, abstract or personalized, which brings moments of vision. Section six concerns problems of reality and illusion, section seven concentrates on the theme of Enlightenment, and the last section on the vast panorama of birth, death and rebirth, however understood, before which the individual drama of the ascent to Enlightenment takes place. The sections, however, must not be regarded as water-tight. Many poems might just as appropriately be placed in more than one position in the collection. The way of ascent is not a road marked out by regular milestones.

As for my inclusions I have drawn equally on all the main spiritual traditions, weighing my choices, where possible, in favour of the unfamiliar. I have consequently excluded such obvious pieces as Wordsworth's 'Tintern Abbey' and Francis Thompson's 'Hound of Heaven': the first because, though I could not exclude the 'Immortality Ode', I have preferred to give extracts from Wordsworth's 'Prelude', and the second because to my ear it rings false. I do not apologize for the presence of much Herbert and Donne. There could have been even more. T. S. Eliot is entirely absent from this book, because he could only have been adequately represented by the inclusion of an entire Quartet, and for this I could not afford the space. As for the poems in foreign languages, I have chosen, on the whole, the more poetic rather than the literal versions. Even so, I am conscious that some of the renderings are rough to the ear. But better a halting translation than none at all. Often I have made my own translations of poems that were either untranslated or, in some cases, I have had the temerity to pass over existing renderings in favour of my own. I have also, in one or two instances, made my own versions of poems that I have found in French or Spanish renderings from languages that I do not know. The selection is entirely personal, and based on sixty or more years of reading.

As for this reading, it has perhaps been overweighted on the side of Spanish and Spanish-American, a field to which I have devoted more than forty years enthusiastic attention. I have also read widely, however, in the other main European languages. If this book is short on Greek, it is because Greek poetry seems to me on the whole unmystical. Such mystical cults as existed in ancient Greece produced little poetry, and they are represented here by a single Orphic inscription. As for the French and German contemporaries of our own Metaphysicals, they are absent, with one or two exceptions, only because I could discover no adequate translations, and do not feel capable of making any myself.

Though my religious beliefs are Buddhist, I do not think that I have allowed this to bias my selection. Adherence to one mystical tradition opens one's eyes to the essential values of all others. Certainly the practice of meditation makes one sensitive to the traces of meditational experience in the writings of other traditions and of some poets who belong to no mystical traditions at all. So to those contemporaries on whom I have drawn, who may think of themselves as far from mystical in their viewpoint, I would say that they are here not because they claim to be writing poetry on mystical themes but because I see in their writing a concern with such themes.

For help with this book, I am, as ever, deeply grateful to my wife for reading me many of the poems; to my son Mark for encouragement and generous help with the organization of the book; and to Mavora Forward for preparing the typescript which, owing to my defective vision, required her close attention.

Upper Basildon, September 1983

PART ONE

The Condition of Humanity

Chorus of Priests

OH wearisome Condition of Humanity!
Borne under one Law, to another bound:
Vainely begot, and yet forbidden vanity;
Created sicke, commanded to be sound:
What meaneth Nature by these diverse Lawes?
Passion and Reason, selfe-division cause:
Is it the marke or Majesty of Power
To make offences that it may forgive?
Nature herselfe doth her owne selfe defloure,
To hate those errours she her selfe doth give.
For how should man thinke that, he may not doe
If Nature did not faile, and punish too?
Tyrant to others, to her selfe unjust,
Only commands things difficult and hard;
Forbids us all things which it knowes is lust,
Makes easie paines, unpossible reward.
If Nature did not take delight in blood,
She would have made more easie wayes to good.
We that are bound by vowes, and by Promotion,
With pompe of holy Sacrifice and rites,
To teach beliefe in good and still devotion,
To preach of Heaven's wonders, and delights:
Yet when each of us in his own heart lookes,
He findes the God there, farre unlike his Bookes.

FULKE GREVILLE, LORD BROOKE

Encounter in Hell

So was it with those squalid visages
    Of demon Cerberus, who roars so loud
    The spirits would fain that deafness gave them ease.
Now passed we on over the shadows bowed
    Beneath the crushing rain, and our feet set
    On seeming bodies that were empty as a cloud.

3

They all lay grovelling prone amid the wet
    Save one who sat up quickly and raised his head,
    Seeing us pass before him, and our eyes met.
'Oh thou who through this drizzling hell art led,'
    He cried out, 'recognize me if thou may'st,
    For thou wast made before I was unmade.'
And I to him: 'The anguish which thou hast
    It may be so obscures thee to my mind
    That 'tis as if for me thou never wast.
But tell me: who art thou in such place confined
    And to such punishment condemned, that though
    Worse may be, none is of so loathsome kind.'

DANTE ALIGHIERI
Inferno, vi. 31–48. Translated from the Italian by Laurence Binyon

Satan's Descent

Which way I fly is hell; myself am hell;
And in the lowest deep a lower deep
Still threat'ning to devour me opens wide,
To which the hell I suffer seems a heav'n.
O then at last relent: is there no place
Left for repentance, none for pardon left?
None left but by submission: and that word
Disdain forbids me, and my dread of shame
Among the Spirits beneath, whom I seduced
With other promises and other vaunts
Than to submit, boasting I could subdue
Th' Omnipotent. Ay me, they little know
How dearly I abide that boast so vain,
Under what torments inwardly I groan;

4

While they adore me on the throne of hell,
With diadem and scepter high advanced,
The lower still I fall, only supreme
In misery; such joy ambition finds.

JOHN MILTON
Paradise Lost, iv. 75–92

Faust's Confession

I, image of the Godhead, who deemed myself but now
On the brink of the mirror of eternal truth and seeing
My rapturous fill of the blaze of clearest Heaven,
Having stripped off my earthly being;
I, more than an angel, I whose boundless urge
To flow through Nature's veins and in the act of creation
To revel it like the gods – what a divination,
What an act of daring – and what an expiation!
One thundering word has swept me over the verge.

To boast myself thine equal I do not dare.
Granted I owned the power to draw thee down,
I lacked the power to hold thee there.
In that blest moment I felt myself,
Felt myself so small, so great;
Cruelly thou didst thrust me back
Into man's uncertain fate.
Who will teach me? What must I shun?
Or must I go where that impulse drives?
Alas, our very actions like our sufferings
Put a brake upon our lives.

J. W. VON GOETHE
Translated from the German by Louis MacNeice

Vision of the City

The City is of Night; perchance of Death,
  But certainly of Night; for never there
Can come the lucid morning's fragrant breath
  After the dewy dawning's cold grey air;
The moon and stars may shine with scorn or pity;
The sun has never visited that city,
  For it dissolveth in the daylight fair.

Dissolveth like a dream of night away;
  Though present in distempered gloom of thought
And deadly weariness of heart all day.
  But when a dream night after night is brought
Throughout a week, and such weeks few or many
Recur each year for several years, can any
  Discern that dream from real life in aught?

For life is but a dream whose shapes return,
  Some frequently, some seldom, some by night
And some by day, some night and day: we learn,
  The while all change and many vanish quite,
In their recurrence with recurrent changes
A certain seeming order; where this ranges
  We count things real; such is memory's might.

JAMES THOMSON
The City of Dreadful Night, I. 1–21

Prayer for Marilyn Monroe

Lord
receive this girl known throughout the whole world as Marilyn Monroe
although this was not her real name
(But you know the real name of this little orphan who was raped at the
    age of nine

6

the young shop-girl who tried to commit suicide at sixteen.)
She appears before You now without any make-up and without her
        press-agent
without photographers and signing no autographs
alone like an astronaut confronting the night of infinite space.
When she was a child (writes TIME magazine) she dreamt that she was
        naked in church
and that a great crowd was bowing before her with their heads touching
        the floor
and that she had to slide out on her bottom so as not to tread on their
        heads.
You know our dreams better than the psychiatrists.
A church, house or cave stands for the safety of the mother's womb
and also something more . . .
the heads, of course, are her fans
(the crowd of heads in the darkness beneath the spotlight).
The church is not the studios of 20th Century-Fox.
The temple – of marble and gold – is the temple of your body,
where the Son of Man stands with a whip in His hand,
driving out the money-changers of 20th Century-Fox,
who made your house of prayer into a thieves' den.
Lord,
in this world, contaminated by sins and radio-activity,
You will not blame a mere shop-girl,
who, like all shop-girls, dreamt of being a film-star.
And her dream became reality (but like reality in technicolour)
She only acted out the script we gave her
– the script of our own lives – And it was an absurd one.
Forgive her, Lord, and forgive us
our 20th Century
and that Colossal Super-Production in which we all worked.
She was hungry for love and we offered her tranquillizers;
for her sadness because men were not saints, she was prescribed
        psycho-analysis.
Remember, Lord, her mounting fear of the camera,
her hatred of make-up – they insisted on fresh make-up for
        every scene –
and how her horror grew continuously,

and she became less and less punctual at the studios.
Like all shop-girls, she dreamt of being a film-star,
and her life was as unreal as a dream interpreted and filed away
      by a psychiatrist.
Her romances were a kiss with her eyes closed,
for when she opened them
she found herself under the studio lights.
Then the studio lights were switched off!
and they took down the two walls of the room (it was a film-set)
while the director went off with his script since the scene
      had been taken
Or they were like a yacht trip, a kiss at Singapore, a ball at Rio,
a reception at the mansion of the Duke and Duchess of Windsor seen
      in the sitting-room of some poor apartment.
The film ended without the final kiss.
They found her dead in bed with her hand on the telephone.
The detectives did not know whom she was going to ring.
Like someone who has dialled the number of an only friend
but instead of his voice merely hears a recorded voice repeating
      WRONG NUMBER.
Or like someone wounded by gangsters
who reaches for a telephone that has been disconnected.
Whoever it may have been she was going to ring
she did not ring (and perhaps it was no one)
or it was Someone whose name is not in the Los Angeles telephone
      directory
            please answer the telephone Lord.

ERNESTO CARDENAL
Translated from the Spanish by J. M. Cohen

On Waking

I wake and feel the fell of dark, not day.
What hours, O what black hours we have spent
This night! what sights you, heart, saw; ways you went!
And more must, in yet longer light's delay.
　　With witness I speak this. But where I say
Hours I mean years, mean life. And my lament
Is cries countless, cries like dead letters sent
To dearest him that lives alas! away.

I am gall, I am heartburn. God's most deep decree
Bitter would have me taste: my taste was me;
Bones built in me, flesh filled, blood brimmed the curse.
　　Selfyeast of spirit a dull dough sours. I see
The lost are like this, and their scourge to be
As I am mine, their sweating selves; but worse.

GERARD MANLEY HOPKINS

Every Day

Every day I rise blindly
to work, in order to live, and I take breakfast
without tasting a drop of it, every morning.
Not knowing whether I have captured, or ever shall,
something that leaps from that savour
or is perhaps only a return of the heart that will lament
until it no longer matters.

The child may believe he is sated with happiness –
What dawns –
our parents' grief that they cannot leave us,
cannot uproot their dreams of love for this world
before them who, like God, out of so much love
believed themselves creators
and maimed us with their love.

9

Fringes of an invisible cloth,
teeth that ferret things out from shortage of feeling, columns
without base or capping,
in a great mouth which has lost the power of speech

Match after match in the dark,
tear after tear in the cloud of dust.

César Vallejo
Translated from the Spanish by J. M: Cohen

Death in Life

How can the tree but waste and wither away
    That hath not sometime comfort of the sun?
How can that flower but fade and soon decay
    That always is with dark clouds over-run?
Is this a life? Nay, death you may it call,
That feels each pain and knows no joy at all.

What foodless beast can live long in good plight?
    Or is it life where senses there be none?
Or what availeth eyes without their light?
    Or else a tongue to him that is alone?
Is this a life? Nay, death you may it call,
That feels each pain and knows no joy at all.

Whereto serve ears if that there be no sound?
    Or such a head where no device doth grow
But all of plaints, since sorrow is the ground
    Whereby the heart doth pine in deadly woe?
Is this a life? Nay, death you may it call,
That feels each pain and knows no joy at all.

Thomas, Lord Vaux

The Expense of Spirit

The expense of spirit in a waste of shame
   Is lust in action; and till action, lust
Is perjured, murderous, bloody, full of blame,
   Savage, extreme, rude, cruel, not to trust;
Enjoyed, no sooner but despisèd straight;
   Past reason hunted; and no sooner had,
Past reason hated, as a swallowed bait,
   On purpose laid to make the taker mad:
Mad in pursuit, and in possession so;
   Had, having, and in quest to have, extreme;
A bliss in proof, and proved, a very woe;
   Before, a joy proposed; behind, a dream.
     All this the world well knows; yet none knows well
     To shun the heaven that leads men to this hell.

WILLIAM SHAKESPEARE

Like Crabs

Like those wounded crabs
that leave their claws on the beach,
so I get rid of my desires,
bite and cut my arms,
prune my days,
dissolve my hope,
destroy myself.
I am on the point of tears.

Where did I lose myself, at what moment
did I come to inhabit my house,
so like myself that even my children take me for their father
and my wife says the usual things to me?

I gather myself piece by piece,
at intervals from the dust-heap of memory,
and try to reconstruct myself,
to make myself like my image,
Nothing, alas, remains!
The dishes slip broken from my hands,
the chairlegs, the soiled pants,
the bones I dug up
and the portraits that show me loves and phantoms.

Take pity on me!
I want to ask someone for pity.
I am going to ask the first person I meet for forgiveness.
I am a stone rolling
because night is on the slope and no one can see the end.
My stomach and my soul ache
and my whole body is waiting in fear
for a kind hand to throw a sheet over me.

JAIME SABINES
Translated from the Spanish by J. M. Cohen

Restless Ambition

How dost thou wear and weary out thy days,
    Restless Ambition, never at an end!
Whose travels no Herculean pillar stays,
    But still beyond thy rest thy labours tend;
Above good fortune thou thy hopes dost raise,
    Still climbing, and yet never canst ascend;
        For when thou hast attained unto the top
        Of thy desires, thou hast not yet got up.

That height of fortune either is controlled
　By some more powerful overlooking eye,
That doth the fulness of thy grace withhold,
　Or counterchecked with some concurrency,
That it doth cost far more ado to hold
　　The height attained, than was to get so high,
　　　Where stand thou canst not, but with careful toil,
　　　Nor loose thy hold without thy utter spoil.

There dost thou struggle with thine own distrust,
　And others' jealousies, their counterplot,
Against some underworking pride, that must
　Supplanted be, or else thou standest not;
There wrong is played with wrong, and he that thrust
　Down others, comes himself to have that lot.
　　The same concussion doth afflict his breast
　　That others shook; oppression is oppressed:

That either happiness dwells not so high,
　Or else above, whereto pride cannot rise;
And that the highest of man's felicity
　But in the region of affliction lies;
And that we climb but up to misery.
　High fortunes are but high calamities.
　　It is not in that sphere, where peace doth move;
　　Rest dwells below it, happiness above.

For in this height of fortune are imbred
　Those thundering fragors that affright the earth;
From thence have all distemperatures their head,
　That brings forth desolation, famine, dearth;
There certain order is disordered,
　And there it is confusion hath her birth.
　　It is that height of fortune doth undo
　　Both her own quietness and others' too.

Samuel Daniel

Life Ephemeral

We come only to sleep, we come only to dream,
It is not true, it is not true that we come to live on earth.

We come to be transformed into the spring grasses,
Our hearts come here to put on fresh green. They come here to
    open their petals.

Our body is a flower, it gives birth to flowers, and it withers.

ANONYMOUS NAHUATL POEM
Adapted from a Spanish version by J. M. Cohen

From The Book of Job

Man that is born of a woman is of few
days, and full of trouble.
He cometh forth like a flower, and is cut
down: he fleeth also as a shadow, and continueth not.
And dost thou open thine eyes upon such
an one, and bringest me into judgment with thee?
Who can bring a clean thing out of an
unclean? not one.
Seeing his days are determined, the
number of his months are with thee, thou
hast appointed his bounds that he cannot
pass;
Turn from him, that he may rest, till he
shall accomplish, as an hireling, his day.
For there is hope of a tree, if it be cut
down, that it will sprout again, and that the
tender branch thereof will not cease.
Though the root thereof wax old in the
earth, and the stock thereof die in the
ground;

14

Yet through the scent of water it will bud,
and bring forth boughs like a plant.

But man dieth, and wasteth away: yea,
man giveth up the ghost, and where is he?

As the waters fail from the sea, and the
flood decayeth and drieth up:

So man lieth down, and riseth not: till
the heavens be no more, they shall not
awake, nor be raised out of their sleep.

Chapter 14. 1–12

The Hell of the Winds

I came into a place of all light dumb
That bellows like a storm in the sea-deep
When the thwart winds that strike it roar and hum.
The abysmal tempest that can never sleep
Snatches the spirits and headlong hurries them,
Beats and besets them with its whirling sweep.
When they arrive before the ruin, stream
The cries up; there the wail is and the moan,
There the divine perfection they blaspheme.
I learnt that in such restless violence blown
This punishment the carnal sinners share
Who let Desire pull Reason from her throne.
And as their beating wings the starlings bear
At the cold season, in broad flocking flight,
So those corrupted spirits were rapt in air
To and fro, down, up, driven in helpless flight,
Comforted by no hope ever to lie
At rest, nor even to bear a pain more light.
And as the cranes in long line streak the sky
And in procession chant their mournful call,

So I saw come with sound of wailing by
The shadows fluttering in the tempest's brawl.
Whereat, 'O Master, who are these,' I said,
'On whom the black winds with their scourges fall?'

DANTE ALIGHIERI
Inferno, v. 28–51. Translated from the Italian by Laurence Binyon

Bill of Sale

God help us, we have sold our souls, all that was best,
To an enterprise in the hands of the Receiver.
We've no dividends, or rights, for the price we paid.
Yet should our wills choose between this corrupt business
And a paradise to come, rest assured they'd want

The world we have now.

ABU-AL-'ALĀ' AL-MA'ARRI
Translated from the Arabic by George Wightman and Abdullah al-Udhari

The Muck Farmer

This man swaying dully before us
Is a muck farmer, to use his own words;
A man unfit to breed the sleek herds,
That win prizes and give the thick milk,
White as the teeth it builds. His rare smile,
Cracked as the windows of his stone house
Sagging under its weight of moss,
Falls on us palely like the wan moon

That cannot pierce the thin cloud
Of March. His speech is a rank garden,
Where thought is choked in the wild tangle
Of vain phrases.
               Leave him, then, crazed and alone
To pleach his dreams with his rough hands.
Our ways have crossed and tend now apart;
Ours to end in a field wisely sown,
His in the mixen of his warped heart.

R. S. THOMAS

The Puppet

By whom was wrought this puppet?
Where is the puppet's maker?
And where does the puppet arise?
Where is the puppet stopped?

Not made by self is this puppet,
Nor is this misfortune made by others.
Conditioned by cause it comes to be,
By breaking of cause is it stopped.

. . . . . .

By whom was wrought this being?
Where is the being's maker?
Where does the being arise?
Where is the being stopped?

Why do you harp on 'being'?
It is a false view for you.
A mere heap of samkharas,* this –
Here no 'being' is got at.

17

For as when the parts are rightly set
We utter the word 'chariot',
So when there are the khandhas† –
By convention, 'there is a being' we say.

For it is simply suffering that comes to be,
Suffering that perishes and wanes,
Not other than suffering comes to be,
Naught else than suffering is stopped.

Samyutta-Nikāya I, 134–35
Translated from the Pali by I. B. Horner

* Samkharas: characteristics
† Khandhas (or skandhas): the constituents of personality

Sonnet on Transience

The brief year sweeps all with it in its train
mocking the brilliant surge of mortal life,
the brave steel and cold marble that in strife
pits its hard strength against time, but in vain.

Before the foot has learnt to walk, it moves
along the road of death, down which I bear
my life, a turgid river, poor and drear,
that the dark sea will swallow in its waves.

Every short moment is a lengthy pace
on that reluctant road, where stage by stage
inert in sleep, we are yet forced to race.

A little breath, a last and bitter pain,
and that is death, our enforced heritage,
not punishment but law. Then why complain?

FRANCISCO DE QUEVEDO
Translated from the Spanish by J. M. Cohen

Eternal Recurrence

Night: the street, a senseless murky
lamp beside a chemist's shop.
You may live on for half a century.
All will be so. There's no escape.

You'll die and start another lifetime.
But all will recur as before.
Night, the canal, its icy ripple,
The street, the lamp at the chemist's door.

ALEXANDER BLOK
Translated from the Russian by J. M. Cohen

The Eighth Duino Elegy

The eyes of all the living creatures see the open.
But *our* eyes are as though reversed
and set around them like encircling traps,
round their free path that leads them outwards.
Our knowledge of what *is* outside
comes to us from the animal's face alone,
for we already turn the young child round and force it
backwards to look at formation – not the open,
so deep within the animal's face. Free from death.
Death we alone see; the free animal
has always its eclipse behind it
and God in front, and when it moves
it moves into eternity, like fountains flowing.
We never have, not for a single day,
pure space before us, into which the flowers
infinitely open. It is always World
and never Nowhere without Not:
the element, unsupervised and pure, one breathes
and infinitely knows and does not covet.
Quietly, a child may lose himself to it,

and then is jerked away. Or someone dies and *is* it.
For close to death one does not see death any more
and stares *beyond*, perhaps as with the animal's wide gaze.
Lovers, if there were not the other who obstructs
the view, draw close to it, and marvel . . .
As if through oversight, behind the other
it is revealed to them . . . But neither can
get past the other, and world returns to them once more.
Always turned towards Creation, all we see
is only a reflection of the open,
darkened by ourselves. Or that a silent animal
raises its gaze which calmly passes through us.
This is what fate means: being opposite,
nothing but that, and always opposite.

If consciousness such as is ours, existed
in the sure animal which on a different course
is coming towards us, he would force us round
with his own movement. But his being
is infinite to him, ungrasped, and with no insight
into his state, pure, like his outward gaze.
Where we see Future he sees Everything,
in Everything himself, for ever whole.

Yet, in the watchfully warm animal
there is the sorrow and the weight of a great sadness.
To him as well, there always clings
what often overwhelms us – a remembrance
as though what we are striving for, had been
already closer, truer, infinitely tender
in its attachment. Here, all is distance,
and there it had been breath. The second home,
after that first one, seems ambiguous and unstable.
O bliss of *little* creatures that *remain*
forever in the womb that brought them forth;
the happiness, o, of the gnat which even when it weds
still leaps *within*: the womb is all.
And see the half-assurance of the bird

which almost, through its origin, knows both,
as if it were the soul of an Etruscan,
of a dead man who rests within a space
but whose recumbent figure on it forms a lid.
And how perplexed a creature is that has to fly,
and issued from a womb. As though it took
fright at itself, it zigzags through the air,
as a crack goes through a cup. The bat's track thus
rends through the porcelain of the evening.

And we: onlookers, always, everywhere,
turned towards it all, and never towards the open!
It overcrowds us. We arrange it, and it loses substance.
We re-arrange it and ourselves lose substance then.

Who has thus turned us round that we,
whatever we may do, are in the attitude
of one who goes away? As he,
on the last hill which once more shows him
all his valley, turns and stops and lingers –
we live, for ever taking leave.

RAINER MARIA RILKE
Translated from the German by Ruth Speirs

The Undeserved Gift

We have planted thorns: shall we gather dates? We
have spun coarse wool: shall we weave fine brocade
therefrom?

Our sins are written down, and we have not erased
them. We have no good works to weigh against our
hateful imperfections.

Our passions are our own destruction. Oh, the bewailings

on the Day of resurrection!

Our life so precious is past and cannot return; and we still are in sin!

How weak and unmanly to sink and settle in this world whereon brave men of God only travel; but make it not their home!

The days of our youth are past: they have been like a night and a day. The night is over, the day is here, but we are not awake.

How long shall we be like a bird perched on the battlement of the house of life? For one day our dust shall be a stone of the battlement.

It would be a wonder if we found shelter on the Day of Judgement: is our soul a shelter unto others to-day?

The bounty of the Master may help us on that Day: but do not think that sins that deserve hell can lead us unto Paradise.

Perchance from the store-house of the grain of grace of the Saints a single ear of corn will be given to us as a gift: we have not sown it ourselves.

SADI
Ode 265. Translated from the Persian; translator unknown

Fear of Death

Ay, but to die, and go we know not where;
To lie in cold obstruction and to rot;
This sensible warm motion to become
A kneaded clod; and the delighted spirit
To bathe in fiery floods, or to reside
In thrilling region of thick-ribbèd ice;
To be imprison'd in the viewless winds
And blown with restless violence round about
The pendant world; or to be worse than worst

Of those that lawless and incertain thoughts
Imagine howling: 'tis too horrible!
The weariest and most loathèd worldly life
That age, ache, penury and imprisonment
Can lay on nature is a paradise
To what we fear of death.

WILLIAM SHAKESPEARE
Measure for Measure, III. ii. 116–30

A Reminder of the End

I saw the ramparts of my native land,
One time so strong, now dropping in decay,
Their strength destroyed by this new age's way,
That has worn out and rotted what was grand.

I went into the fields: there I could see
The sun drink up the waters newly thawed,
And on the hills the moaning cattle pawed;
Their miseries robbed the day of light for me.

I went into my house: I saw how spotted,
Decaying things made that old home their prize.
My withered walking-staff had come to bend.
I felt the age had won; my sword was rotted,
And there was nothing on which to set my eyes
That was not a reminder of the end.

FRANCISCO DE QUEVEDO
Translated from the Spanish by John Masefield

The Golden Goose Speaks

To remain from birth to death without the Good Law,
  – that prolongs the bondage.
To desire emancipation, and still deserve a state of
  woe, – that prolongs the bondage.
To hope for miraculous blessings, and still have
  wrong opinions, – that prolongs the bondage.
To neglect those things which turn the mind
  towards salvation, – that prolongs the bondage.
To strive for purity of vision, and yet be blinded
  by a faulty judgment, – that prolongs the bondage.
To give and yet be checked by meanness,
  – that prolongs the bondage.
To aim at lasting achievements while still exposed
  to this world's distractions, – that prolongs the bondage.
To try to understand one's inner mind
  while still chained to hopes and fears,
  – that prolongs the bondage.

The Buddha's Law among the Birds
Translated from the Tibetan by Edward Conze

The Second Coming

Turning and turning in the widening gyre
The falcon cannot hear the falconer;
Things fall apart; the centre cannot hold;
Mere anarchy is loosed upon the world,
The blood-dimmed tide is loosed, and everywhere
The ceremony of innocence is drowned;
The best lack all conviction, while the worst
Are full of passionate intensity.

Surely some revelation is at hand;
Surely the Second Coming is at hand.
The Second Coming! Hardly are those words out
When a vast image out of Spiritus Mundi
Troubles my sight: somewhere in sands of the desert
A shape with lion body and the head of a man,
A gaze blank and pitiless as the sun,
Is moving its slow thighs, while all about it
Reel shadows of the indignant desert birds.
The darkness drops again; but now I know
That twenty centuries of stony sleep
Were vexed to nightmare by a rocking cradle,
And what rough beast, its hour come round at last,
Slouches towards Bethlehem to be born?

W. B. YEATS

To Jesus Christ

Thy followers today are less like Thee,
The crucified, than those who made Thee die,
Good Jesus, wandering all ways awry
From rules prescribed in Thy wise charity.
The saints now most esteemed love lying lips,
Lust, strife, injustice; sweet to them the cry
Drawn forth by monstrous pangs from men that die:
So many plagues hath not the Apocalypse
As these wherewith they smite Thy friends ignored
Even as I am; search my heart, and know;
My life, my sufferings bear Thy stamp and sign.
If Thou return to earth, come armed; for lo,
Thy foes prepare fresh crosses for Thee, Lord!
Not Turks, not Jews, but they who call them Thine.

TOMASO CAMPANELLA
Translated from the Italian by J. A. Symonds

25

From Lamentations

How doth the city sit solitary, that was
full of people! how is she become as
a widow! she that was great among the
nations, and princess among the provinces,
how is she become tributary!

She weepeth sore in the night, and her
tears are on her cheeks: among all her
lovers she hath none to comfort her: all
her friends have dealt treacherously with
her, they are become her enemies.

Judah is gone into captivity because of
affliction, and because of great servitude:
she dwelleth among the heathen, she findeth
no rest: all her persecutors overtook her
between the straits.

The ways of Zion do mourn, because
none come to the solemn feasts: all her
gates are desolate: her priests sigh, her
virgins are afflicted, and she is in bitterness.

Her adversaries are the chief, her enemies
prosper; for the LORD hath afflicted her for
the multitude of her transgressions: her
children are gone into captivity before the
enemy.

And from the daughter of Zion all her
beauty is departed: her princes are become
like harts that find no pasture, and they
are gone without strength before the pursuer.

Jerusalem remembered in the days of her
affliction and of her miseries all her pleasant
things that she had in the days of old, when
her people fell into the hand of the enemy,
and none did help her: the adversaries saw
her, and did mock at her sabbaths.

Jerusalem hath grievously sinned; therefore she is removed: all that honoured her despise her, because they have seen her nakedness: yea, she sigheth, and turneth backward.

Chapter I. 1–8

PART TWO

You Yet but Knock

On the Flightiness of Thought

Shame to my thoughts, how they stray from me!
I fear great danger from it on the day of eternal Doom.

During the psalms they wander on a path that is not right:
They flash, they fret, they misbehave before the eyes of great
   God.

Through eager crowds, through companies of wanton
      women,
Through woods, through cities – swifter they are than the
   wind.

Now through paths of loveliness, anon of riotous shame!

Without a ferry or ever missing a step they go across every
      sea:
Swiftly they leap in one bound from earth to heaven.

They run a race of folly anear and afar:
After a course of giddiness they return to their home.

Though one should try to bind them or put shackles on their
      feet,
They are neither constant nor mindful to take a spell of rest.

Neither sword-edge nor crack of whip will keep them down
      strongly:
As slippery as an eel's tail they glide out of my grasp.

Neither lock nor firm-vaulted dungeon nor any fetter on
      earth,
Stronghold nor sea nor bleak fastness restrains them from
   their course.

O beloved truly chaste Christ to whom every eye is clear,
May the grace of the seven-fold Spirit come to keep them, to
   check them!

Rule this heart of mine. O dread God of the elements,
That Thou mayst be my love, that I may do Thy will.

That I may reach Christ with His chosen companions, that
    we may be together!
They are neither fickle nor inconstant – not as I am.

ANONYMOUS
Translated from the Irish by Kuno Meyer

If Thy Soul is a Stranger to Thee

I laugh when I hear that the fish in the water is thirsty.
Perceivest thou not how the god is in thine own house,
    that thou wanderest from forest to forest so listlessly?
In thy home is the Truth. Go where thou wilt, to Benares
    or to Mathura;
    if thy soul is a stranger to thee, the whole world is
        unhomely.

KABIR
Translated from the Hindi by Rabindranath Tagore and revised by
Robert Bridges

Psalm 53

The fool hath said in his heart, There is no God.
Corrupt are they, and have done abominable iniquity:
there is none that doeth good.
    God looked down from heaven upon the children of men,
to see if there were any that did understand, that did
seek God.

Every one of them is gone back: they are altogether
become filthy; there is none that doeth good, no, not one.
Have the workers of iniquity no knowledge? who eat up
my people as they eat bread: they have not called upon God.
There were they in great fear, where no fear was: for
God hath scattered the bones of him that encampeth against
thee: thou has put them to shame, because God hath
despised them.
Oh that the salvation of Israel were come out of Zion!
When God bringeth back the captivity of his people, Jacob
shall rejoice, and Israel shall be glad.

Vanity of Vanity

The fables of the world have filched away
The time I had for thinking upon God;
His grace lies buried 'neath oblivious sod,
Whence springs an evil crop of sins alway.
What makes another wise, leads me astray,
Slow to discern the bad path I have trod:
Hope fades; but still desire ascends that God
May free me from self-love, my sure decay.
Shorten halfway my road to heaven from earth!
Dear Lord, I cannot even halfway rise,
Unless Thou help me on this pilgrimage.
Teach me to hate the world so little worth,
And all the lovely things I clasp and prize;
That endless life, ere death, may be my wage.

MICHELANGELO BUONARROTI
Translated from the Italian by J. A. Symonds

Poor Soul

Poor soul, the centre of my sinful earth,
   Feeding these rebel powers that thee array,
Why dost thou pine within and suffer dearth,
   Painting thy outward walls so costly gay?
Why so large cost, having so short a lease,
   Dost thou upon thy fading mansion spend?
Shall worms, inheritors of this excess,
   Eat up thy charge? Is this thy body's end?
Then, soul, live thou upon thy servant's loss,
   And let that pine to aggravate thy store;
Buy terms divine in selling hours of dross;
    Within be fed, without be rich no more:
      So shalt thou feed on Death, that feeds on men,
      And Death once dead, there's no more dying then.

WILLIAM SHAKESPEARE

The Soul's Apology

Six thousand years or more on earth I've been:
Witness those histories of nations dead,
Which for our age I have illustrated
In philosophic volumes, scene by scene.
And thou, mere mite, seeing my sun serene
Eclipsed, will argue that I had no head
To live by. – Why not try the sun instead,
If nought in fate unfathomed thou hast seen?
If wise men, whom the world rebukes, combined
With tyrant wolves, brute beasts we should become.
The sage, once stoned for sin, you canonise.
When rennet melts, much milk makes haste to bind.
The more you blow the flames, the more they rise,
Bloom into stars, and find in heaven their home.

TOMASO CAMPANELLA
Translated from the Italian by J. A. Symonds

34

Psalm 130

Out of the depths have I cried unto thee, O Lord.
Lord, hear my voice: let thine ears be attentive to
the voice of my supplications.
If thou, Lord, shouldest mark iniquities, O Lord, who
shall stand?
But there is forgiveness with thee, that thou mayest
be feared.
I wait for the Lord, my soul doth wait, and in his
word do I hope.
My soul waiteth for the Lord more than they that watch
for the morning: I say, more than they that watch for
the morning.
Let Israel hope in the Lord: for with the Lord there
is mercy, and with him is plenteous redemption.
And he shall redeem Israel from all his iniquities.

A Hymn to God the Father

Wilt thou forgive that sinne where I begunne,
　　Which is my sin, though it were done before?
Wilt thou forgive those sinnes, through which I runne,
　　And do run still: though still I do deplore?
　　　　When thou hast done, thou hast not done,
　　　　　　For, I have more.

Wilt thou forgive, that sinne by which I have wonne
　　Others to sinne? and, made my sinne their doore?
Wilt thou forgive that sinne which I did shunne
　　A yeare, or two, but wallowed in, a score?
　　　　When thou hast done, thou hast not done,
　　　　　　For I have more.

I have a sin of feare, that when I have spunne
My last thred, I shall perish on the shore;
Sweare by thy selfe that at my death, thy sonne
Shall shine as he shines now, and heretofore;
And, having done that, Thou haste done,
I feare no more.

JOHN DONNE

Hope for Forgiveness

No good works have I done in my life: my life has
in truth been lost in wantonness.

What hope shall I have at the hour of Resurrection?
Only the hope that God may forgive me.

How many the sufferings of a soul on that day! Of
a soul that has not been pure.

How I wish sometimes that the day of Judgement was
not! That sins and good works should not be remembered.

But sometimes I think it is wrong to despair: cannot
God in his bounty forgive me?

My eyes cannot see the right path: forgive me, my
God, or set a lamp before my feet through thy mercy.

In the shame of my sins my head is bowed down:
bid me to raise it, and I will raise it unto the highest
heaven.

Great has been my disobedience, and innumerable
are my sins: and yet I hope for forgiveness.

O my God! What work of Sadi shall be good in
thy sight? Give me the power to do it: or forgive my
weakness.

SADI
Ode 200. Translated from the Persian; translator unknown

Dulnesse

Why do I languish thus, drooping and dull,
       As if I were all earth?
O give me quicknesse, that I may with mirth
       Praise thee brim-full!

The wanton lover in a curious strain
       Can praise his fairest fair;
And with quaint metaphors her curled hair
       Curl o'er again.

Thou art my lovelinesse, my life, my light,
       Beautie alone to me:
Thy bloudy death and undeserv'd, makes thee
       Pure red and white.

When all perfections as but one appeare,
       That those thy form doth show,
The very dust, where thou dost tread and go,
       Makes beauties here.

Where are my lines then? my approaches? views?
       Where are my window-songs?
Lovers are still pretending, & ev'n wrongs
       Sharpen their Muse:

But I am lost in flesh, whose sugred lyes
       Still mock me, and grow bold:
Sure thou didst put a minde there, if I could
       Finde where it lies.

Lord, cleare thy gift, that with a constant wit
       I may but look towards thee:
Look onely; for to love thee, who can be,
       What angel fit?

GEORGE HERBERT

When As Mans Life

When as Mans life, the light of human lust,
In socket of his earthly lanthorne burnes,
That all this glory unto ashes must,
And generation to corruption turnes;
    Then fond desires that onely feare their end,
    Doe vainely wish for life, but to amend.
But when this life is from the body fled,
To see it selfe in that *eternall Glasse,*
Where time doth end, and thoughts accuse the dead,
Where all to come, is one with all that was;
    Then living men aske how he left his breath,
    That while he lived never thought of death.

FULKE GREVILLE, LORD BROOKE

Who Shall Deliver Me?

God strengthen me to bear myself;
That heaviest weight of all to bear,
Inalienable weight of care.

All others are outside myself;
I lock my door and bar them out,
The turmoil, tedium, gad-about.

I lock my door upon myself,
And bar them out; but who shall wall
Self from myself, most loathed of all?

If I could once lay down myself,
And start self-purged upon the race
That all must run! Death runs apace.

If I could set aside myself,
And start with lightened heart upon
The road by all men overgone!

God harden me against myself,
This coward with pathetic voice
Who craves for ease, and rest, and joys:

Myself, arch-traitor to myself;
My hollowest friend, my deadliest foe,
My clog whatever road I go.

Yet One there is can curb myself,
Can roll the strangling load from me,
Break off the yoke and set me free.

CHRISTINA ROSSETTI

Hymn to God my God, in my Sicknesse

Since I am coming to that Holy roome,
   Where, with thy Quire of Saints for evermore,
I shall be made thy Musique; As I come
   I tune the Instrument here at the dore,
   And what I must doe then, thinke here before.

Whilst my Physitians by their love are growne
   Cosmographers, and I their Mapp, who lie
Flat on this bed, that by them may be showne
   That this is my South-west discoverie
   Per fretum febris, by these streights to die,

I joy, that in these straits, I see my West;
   For though their currents yeeld returne to none,
What shall my West hurt me? As West and East
   In all flat Maps (and I am one) are one,
   So death doth touch the Resurrection.

Is the Pacifique Sea my home? Or are
  The Easterne riches? Is *Jerusalem*?
Anyan, and *Magellan*, and *Gibraltare*,
  All streights, and none but streights, are wayes to them,
  Whether where *Japhet* dwelt, or *Cham*, or *Sem*.

We thinke that *Paradise* and *Calvarie*,
  Christs Crosse, and *Adams* tree, stood in one place;
Looke Lord, and finde both *Adams* met in me;
  As the first *Adams* sweat surrounds my face,
  May the last *Adams* blood my soule embrace.

So, in his purple wrapp'd receive mee Lord,
  By these his thornes give me his other Crowne;
And as to other soules I preach'd thy word,
  Be this my Text, my Sermon to mine owne,
  Therefore that he may raise the Lord throws down.

JOHN DONNE

At The Foot of the Cross

Freed from a burden sore and grievous band,
Dear Lord, and from this wearying world untied,
Like a frail bark I turn me to Thy side,
As from a fierce storm to a tranquil land.
Thy thorns, Thy nails, and either bleeding hand,
With Thy mild gentle piteous face, provide
Promise of help and mercies multiplied,
And hope that yet my soul secure may stand.
Let not Thy holy eyes be just to see
My evil past, Thy chastened ears to hear
And stretch the arm of judgment to my crime:

40

Let Thy blood only lave and succour me,
Yielding more perfect pardon, better cheer,
As older still I grow with lengthening time.

MICHELANGELO BUONARROTI
Translated from the Italian by J. A. Symonds

Batter My Heart

Batter my heart, three person'd God; for, you
As yet but knocke, breathe, shine, and seeke to mend;
That I may rise, and stand, o'erthrow mee,' and bend
Your force, to breake, blowe, burn and make me new.
I, like an usurpt towne, to' another due,
Labour to' admit you, but Oh, to no end,
Reason your viceroy in mee, mee should defend,
But is captiv'd, and proves weake or untrue.
Yet dearely' I love you, and would be lov'd faine,
But am betroth'd unto your enemie:
Divorce mee,' untie, or breake that knot againe,
Take mee to you, imprison mee, for I
Except you' enthrall mee, never shall be free,
Nor ever chast, except you ravish mee.

JOHN DONNE

Thou Art Indeed Just

Thou art indeed just, Lord, if I contend
With thee; but, sir, so what I plead is just.
Why do sinners' ways prosper? and why must
Disappointment all I endeavour end?
  Wert thou my enemy, O thou my friend,

41

How wouldst thou worse, I wonder, than thou dost
Defeat, thwart me? Oh, the sots and thralls of lust
Do in spare hours more thrive than I that spend,
Sir, life upon thy cause. See, banks and brakes
Now, leavèd how thick! lacèd they are again
With fretty chervil, look, and fresh wind shakes
Them; birds build – but not I build; no, but strain,
Time's eunuch, and not breed one work that wakes.
Mine, O thou lord of life, send my roots rain.

GERARD MANLEY HOPKINS

To a Friend with a Religious Vocation
For C.

Thinking of your vocation, I am filled
With thoughts of my own lack of one. I see
Within myself no wish to breed or build
Or take the three vows ringed by poverty.
    And yet I have a sense,
Vague and inchoate, with no symmetry,
Of purpose. Is it merely a pretence,

A kind of scaffolding which I erect
Half out of fear, half out of laziness?
The fitful poems come but can't protect
The empty areas of loneliness.
    You know what you must do,
So that mere breathing is a way to bless.
Dark nights, perhaps, but no grey days for you.

Your vows enfold you. I must make my own;
Now this, now that, each one empirical.
My poems move from feelings not yet known,
And when the poem is written I can feel
    A flash, a moment's peace.
The curtain will be drawn across your grille.
My silences are always enemies.

Yet with the same convictions that you have
(It is but your vocation that I lack),
I must, like you, believe in perfect love.
It is the dark, the dark that draws me back
    Into a chaos where
Vocations, visions fail, the will grows slack
And I am stunned by silence everywhere.

ELIZABETH JENNINGS

De Profundis

Out of these depths:

Where footsteps wander in the marsh of death and an
Intense infernal glare is on our faces facing down:

Out of these depths, what shamefaced cry
Half choked in the dry throat, as though a stone
Were our confounded tongue, can ever rise:
Because the mind has been struck blind
And may no more conceive
Thy Throne.

Because the depths
Are clear with only death's
Marsh-light, because the rock of grief
Is clearly too extreme for us to breach:
Deepen our depths,

And aid our unbelief.

DAVID GASCOYNE

Lachrimae Coactae

Crucified Lord, however much I burn
to be enamoured of your paradise,
knowing what ceases and what will not cease,
frightened of hell, not knowing where to turn,

I fall between harsh grace and hurtful scorn.
You are the crucified who crucifies,
self-withdrawn even from your own device,
your trim-plugged body, wreath of rakish thorn.

What grips me then, or what does my soul grasp?
If I grasp nothing what is there to break?
You are beyond me, innermost true light,

uttermost exile for no exile's sake,
king of our earth not caring to unclasp
its void embrace, the semblance of your quiet.

GEOFFREY HILL

Voice

I walk on the sea-shore
to catch that voice
between the breaking of one wave
and another

but there is no voice
only the senile garrulity of water
salty nothing
a white bird's wing
stuck dry to a stone

I walk to the forest
where persists the continuous
hum of an immense hour-glass
sifting leaves into humus
humus into leaves
powerful jaws of insects
consume the silence of the earth

I walk into the fields
green and yellow sheets
fastened with pins of insects beings
sing at every touch of the wind

where is that voice
it should speak up
when for a moment there is a pause
in the unrelenting monologue of the earth

nothing but whispers
clappings explosions

I come home
and my experience takes on
the shape of an alternative
either the world is dumb
or I am deaf

but perhaps
we are both
doomed to our afflictions

therefore we must
arm in arm
go blindly on
towards new horizons
towards contracted throats
from which rises
an unintelligible gurgle.

ZBIGNIEW HERBERT
Translated from the Polish by Czeslaw Milosz and Peter Dale Scott

Why Are Wee by All Creatures Waited On?

Why are wee by all creatures waited on?
Why doe the prodigall elements supply
Life and food to mee, being more pure then I,
Simple, and further from corruption?
Why brook'st thou, ignorant horse, subjection?
Why dost thou bull, and bore so seelily
Dissemble weaknesse, and by' one mans stroke die,
Whose whole kinde, you might swallow and feed upon?
Weaker I am, woe is mee, and worse then you,
You have not sinn'd, nor need be timorous.
But wonder at a greater wonder, for to us
Created nature doth these things subdue,
But their Creator, whom sin, nor nature tyed,
For us, his Creatures, and his foes, hath dyed.

JOHN DONNE

On His Blindness

When I consider how my light is spent,
  Ere half my days, in this dark world and wide,
  And that one Talent which is death to hide,
  Lodg'd with me useless, though my Soul more bent
To serve therewith my Maker, and present
  My true account, lest he returning chide,
  Doth God exact day-labour, light deny'd,
  I fondly ask; But patience to prevent
That murmur, soon replies, God doth not need
  Either man's work or his own gifts, who best
  Bear his milde yoak, they serve him best, his State
Is Kingly. Thousands at his bidding speed
  And post o'er Land and Ocean without rest:
  They also serve who only stand and waite.

JOHN MILTON

In Honour of St Alphonsus Rodriguez
Lay brother of the Society of Jesus

Honour is flashed off exploit, so we say;
And those strokes once that gashed flesh or galled shield
Should tongue that time now, trumpet now that field,
And, on the fighter, forge his glorious day.
On Christ they do and on the martyr may;
But be the war within, the brand we wield
Unseen, the heroic breast not outward-steeled,
Earth hears no hurtle then from fiercest fray.

  Yet God (that hews mountain and continent,
Earth, all, out; who, with trickling increment,
Veins violets and tall trees makes more and more)
Could crowd career with conquest while there went
Those years and years by of world without event
That in Majorca Alfonso watched the door.

GERARD MANLEY HOPKINS

47

Kyrie

Is man's destructive lust insatiable? There is
Grief in the blow that shatters the innocent face.
Pain blots out clearer sense. And pleasure suffers
The trial thrust of death in even the bride's embrace.

The black catastrophe that can lay waste our worlds
May be unconsciously desired. Fear masks our face;
And tears as warm and cruelly wrung as blood
Are tumbling even in the mouth of our grimace.

How can our hope ring true? Fatality of guilt
And complicated anguish confounds time and place;
While from the tottering ancestral house an angry voice
Resounds in prophecy. Grant us extraordinary grace,

O spirit hidden in the dark in us and deep,
And bring to light the dream out of our sleep.

DAVID GASCOYNE

Lachrimae Amantis

What is there in my heart that you should sue
so fiercely for its love? What kind of care
brings you as though a stranger to my door
through the long night and in the icy dew

seeking the heart that will not harbour you,
that keeps itself religiously secure?
At this dark solstice filled with frost and fire
your passion's ancient wounds must bleed anew.

So many nights the angel of my house
had fed such urgent comfort through a dream,
whispered 'your lord is coming, he is close'

that I have drowsed half-faithful for a time
bathed in pure tones of promise and remorse:
'tomorrow I shall wake to welcome him.'

GEOFFREY HILL

The Collar

I struck the board, and cry'd, No more.
                    I will abroad.
What? shall I ever sigh and pine?
My lines and life are free; free as the rode,
    Loose as the winde, as large as store.
            Shall I be still in suit?
Have I no harvest but a thorn
To let me bloud, and not restore
What I have lost with cordiall fruit?
                    Sure there was wine
        Before my sighs did drie it: there was corn
        Before my tears did drown it.
    Is the yeare onely lost to me?
        Have I no bayes to crown it?
No flowers, no garlands gay? all blasted?
                    All wasted?
    Not so, my heart: but there is fruit,
            And thou hast hands.
        Recover all thy sigh-blown age
On double pleasures: leave thy cold dispute
Of what is fit, and not. Forsake thy cage,
            Thy rope of sands,
Which pettie thoughts have made, and made to thee
    Good cable, to enforce and draw,
            And be thy law,

49

While thou didst wink and wouldst not see.
Away; take heed:
I will abroad.
Call in thy deaths head there: tie up thy fears.
He that forbears
To suit and serve his need,
Deserves his load.
But as I rav'd and grew more fierce and wilde
At every word,
Me thoughts I heard one calling, *Child*:
And I reply'd, *My Lord*.

George Herbert

My Own Heart

My own heart let me more have pity on; let
Me live to my sad self hereafter kind,
Charitable; not live this tormented mind
With this tormented mind tormenting yet.
    I cast for comfort I can no more get
By groping round my comfortless, than blind
Eyes in their dark can day or thirst can find
Thirst's all-in-all in all a world of wet.

Soul, self; come, poor Jackself, I do advise
You, jaded, let be; call off thoughts awhile
Elsewhere; leave comfort root-room; let joy size
At God knows when to God knows what; whose smile
's not wrung, see you; unforeseen times rather – as skies
Betweenpie mountains – lights a lovely mile.

Gerard Manley Hopkins

A Prayer for Good Behaviour

Let us beseech God to help us to self-control: he
  who lacks self-control is deprived of the grace of the Lord.
The undisciplined man does not corrupt himself alone: he
  sets the whole world afire.
Whatever befalls thee of gloom and sorrow is the result of
  thy irreverence and insolence.
Any one behaving with irreverence in the path of the
  Friend is a brigand who robs men: he is no man.
Through discipline Heaven was filled with light, through
  discipline the Angels became immaculate and holy.
By reason of irreverence the sun is eclipsed, and insolence
  caused 'Azāzīl to be turned back from the door.

From the *Mathnawī* of RŪMĪ
Translated from the Persian by R. A. Nicholson

The Four Ages of Man

He with body waged a fight,
But body won; it walks upright.

Then he struggled with the heart;
Innocence and peace depart.

Then he struggled with the mind;
His proud heart he left behind.

Now his wars on God begin;
At stroke of midnight God shall win.

W. B. YEATS

Green Categories

You never heard of Kant, did you, Prytherch?
A strange man! What would he have said
Of your life here, free from the remote
War of antinomies; free also
From mind's uncertainty faced with a world
Of its own making?
                             Here all is sure;
Things exist rooted in the flesh,
Stone, tree and flower. Even while you sleep
In your low room, the dark moor exerts
Its pressure on the timbers. Space and time
Are not the mathematics that your will
Imposes, but a green calendar
Your heart observes; how else could you
Find your way home or know when to die
With the slow patience of the men who raised
This landmark in the moor's deep tides?

His logic would have failed; your mind, too,
Exposed suddenly to the cold wind
Of genius, faltered. Yet at night together
In your small garden, fenced from the wild moor's
Constant aggression, you could have been at one,
Sharing your faith over a star's blue fire.

R. S. THOMAS

From In Memoriam

That which we dare invoke to bless;
    Our dearest faith; our ghastliest doubt;
    He, They, One, All; within, without;
The Power in darkness whom we guess;

I found Him not in world or sun,
　Or eagle's wing, or insect's eye;
　Nor thro' the questions men may try,
The petty cobwebs we have spun:

If e'er when faith had fall'n asleep,
　I heard a voice 'believe no more'
　And heard an ever-breaking shore
That tumbled in the Godless deep;

A warmth within the breast would melt
　The freezing reason's colder part,
　And like a man in wrath the heart
Stood up and answer'd 'I have felt.'

No, like a child in doubt and fear:
　But that blind clamour made me wise;
　Then was I as a child that cries,
But, crying, knows his father near;

And what I am beheld again
　What is, and no man understands;
　And out of darkness came the hands
That reach thro' nature, moulding men.

ALFRED, LORD TENNYSON

The Eclipse

I stood out in the open cold
To see the essence of the eclipse
Which was its perfect darkness.

I stood in the cold on the porch
And could not think of anything so perfect
As man's hope of light in the face of darkness.

RICHARD EBERHART

PART THREE

The Inward Eye

Daffodils

I wandered lonely as a cloud
    That floats on high o'er vales and hills,
When all at once I saw a crowd,
    A host, of golden daffodils;
Beside the lake, beneath the trees,
Fluttering and dancing in the breeze.

Continuous as the stars that shine
    And twinkle on the Milky Way,
They stretched in never-ending line
    Along the margin of a bay:
Ten thousand saw I at a glance,
Tossing their heads in sprightly dance.

The waves beside them danced, but they
    Out-did the sparkling waves in glee:
A poet could not but be gay
    In such a jocund company:
I gazed – and gazed – but little thought
What wealth the show to me had brought:

For oft, when on my couch I lie
    In vacant or in pensive mood,
They flash upon that inward eye
    Which is the bliss of solitude;
And then my heart with pleasure fills,
And dances with the daffodils.

WILLIAM WORDSWORTH

Wynter Wakeneth

Wynter wakeneth al my care;
Nou this leves waxeth bare;
Ofte I sike and mourne sare,
   When hit cometh in my thoght
Of this worldes ioie, hou hit geth al to noht.

Nou hit is, and nou hit nys,
Also hit ner nere ywys.
That moni man seith, soth hit is,
    Al goth bote Godès wille.
Allè we shulè deye, thah us like ylle.

Al that gren me greveth grene,
Now hit faleueth al by dene.
Jesu, help that hit be sene,
    Ant shild us from helle,
For I not whider I shal, ne hou longe her duelle!

ANONYMOUS

Vision of Eden

Another side, umbrageous Grots and Caves
Of coole recess, o'er which the mantling Vine
Layes forth her purple Grape, and gently creeps
Luxuriant; mean while murmuring waters fall
Down the slope hills, disperst, or in a Lake,
That to the fringed Bank with Myrtle crownd,
Her chrystall mirror holds, unite thir streams.
The Birds thir quire apply; aires, vernal aires,
Breathing the smell of field and grove, attune
The trembling leaves, while Universal *Pan*
Knit with the *Graces* and the *Hours* in dance
Led on th'Eternal Spring. Not that faire field
Of *Enna*, where *Proserpin* gathring flours
Her self a fairer Flowre by gloomie *Dis*
Was gatherd, which cost *Ceres* all that pain
To seek her through the world; nor that sweet Grove
Of *Daphne* by *Orontes*, and th'inspir'd
Castalian Spring might with this Paradise
Of *Eden* strive.

JOHN MILTON
Paradise Lost, iv. 257-75

58

The Winter Walk at Noon

The night was winter in his roughest mood;
The morning sharp and clear. But now at noon
Upon the southern side of the slant hills,
And where the woods fence off the northern blast,
The season smiles, resigning all its rage,
And has the warmth of May. The vault is blue
Without a cloud, and white without a speck
The dazzling splendour of the scene below.
Again the harmony comes o'er the vale;
And through the trees I view th' embattled tower
Whence all the music. I again perceive
The soothing influence of the wafted strains,
And settle in soft musings as I tread
The walk, still verdant, under oaks and elms,
Whose outspread branches overarch the glade.
The roof, though moveable through all its length
As the wind sways it, has yet well sufficed,
And, intercepting in their silent fall
The frequent flakes, has kept a path for me.
No noise is here, or none that hinders thought.
The redbreast warbles still, but is content
With slender notes, and more than half suppress'd;
Pleased with his solitude, and flitting light
From spray to spray, where'er he rests he shakes
From many a twig the pendent drops of ice
That tinkle in the wither'd leaves below.
Stillness, accompanied with sounds so soft,
Charms more than silence. Meditation here
May think down hours to moments. Here the heart
May give a useful lesson to the head,
And Learning wiser grow without his books
Knowledge and Wisdom, far from being one,
Have ofttimes no connexion. Knowledge dwells
In heads replete with thoughts of other men;
Wisdom in minds attentive to their own.

WILLIAM COWPER

Säntis: Winter

Through powdered snow and reeking mist
At length there breaks a cloudless day.
Then every window is thrown up,
And each discovers what he may.

Can they be houses, those great shapes?
Is it a pond, that level patch?
The belfry, in that uniform,
Is hard to recognize as such.

And all life lies beneath a weight,
Smothered as in a winding-sheet.
But look, in the horizon's haze
The living earth confronts my gaze!

Grim warder, let the south wind go
From your cold dungeon down below.
Where those white crests show black between,
There he must pass the quarantine,
The foreigner from Lombardy.
O Säntis, set the warm wind free.

ANNETTE VON DROSTE-HÜLSHOFF
Translated from the German by J. M. Cohen

The Angle of a Landscape

The Angle of a Landscape –
That every time I wake –
Between my Curtain and the Wall
Upon an ample Crack –

Like a Venetian – waiting –
Accosts my open eye –
Is just a Bough of Apples –
Held slanting, in the Sky –

The Pattern of a Chimney –
The Forehead of a Hill –
Sometimes – a Vane's Forefinger –
But that's – Occasional –

The Seasons – shift – my Picture –
Upon my Emerald Bough,
I wake – to find no – Emeralds –
Then – Diamonds – which the Snow

From Polar Caskets – fetched me –
The Chimney – and the Hill –
And just the Steeple's finger –
These – never stir at all –

EMILY DICKINSON

Going Alone to Spend a Night at the Hsien-Yu Temple

The crane from the shore standing at the top of the steps
The moon on the pool seen at the open door;
Where these are, I made my lodging-place
And for two nights could not turn away.
I am glad I chanced on a place so lonely and still
With no companion to drag me early home.
Now that I have tasted the joy of being alone,
I will never again come with a friend at my side.

PO CHÜ-I
Translated from the Chinese by Arthur Waley

The Mountain Boat

One summer evening (led by her) I found
A little boat tied to a willow tree
Within a rocky cave, its usual home.
Straight I unloosed her chain, and stepping in
Pushed from the shore. It was an act of stealth
And troubled pleasure, nor without the voice
Of mountain-echoes did my boat move on;
Leaving behind her still, on either side,
Small circles glittering idly in the moon,
Until they melted all into one track
Of sparkling light. But now, like one who rows,
Proud of his skill, to reach a chosen point
With an unswerving line, I fixed my view
Upon the summit of a craggy ridge,
The horizon's utmost boundary; for above
Was nothing but the stars and the grey sky.
She was an elfin pinnace; lustily
I dipped my oars into the silent lake,
And, as I rose upon the stroke, my boat
Went heaving through the water like a swan;
When, from behind that craggy steep till then
The horizon's bound, a huge peak, black and huge,
As if with voluntary power instinct
Upreared its head. I struck and struck again,
And growing still in stature the grim shape
Towered up between me and the stars, and still,
For so it seemed, with purpose of its own
And measured motion like a living thing,
Strode after me. With trembling oars I turned,
And through the silent water stole my way
Back to the covert of the willow tree;
There in her mooring-place I left my bark, –
And through the meadows homeward went, in grave
And serious mood; but after I had seen
That spectacle, for many days, my brain
Worked with a dim and undetermined sense
Of unknown modes of being; o'er my thoughts
There hung a darkness, call it solitude

Or blank desertion. No familiar shapes
Remained, no pleasant images of trees,
Of sea or sky, no colours of green fields;
But huge and mighty forms, that do not live
Like living men, moved slowly through the mind
By day, and were a trouble to my dreams.

WILLIAM WORDSWORTH
The Prelude, I. 357–400

Question and Answer Among the Mountains

You ask me why I dwell in the green mountain;
I smile and make no reply for my heart is free of care.
As the peach-blossom flows down stream and is gone into
    the unknown,
I have a world apart that is not among men.

LI-PO
Translated from the Chinese by Robert Kotewall and Norman L. Smith

Mountain Temple

I have locked the gate on a thousand peaks
To live here with clouds and birds.
All day I watch the hills
As clear winds fill the bamboo door.
A supper of pine flowers,
Monk's robes of chestnut dye –
What dream does the world hold
To lure me from these dark slopes?

ZEKKAI
Translated from the Chinese by Burton Watson

Potters of the T'ang

They need no words for, if they wish
To utter forms that burn for birth,
They throw, fire, cool their pots,
And meet
In silence when with bows,
With hands outstretched
That deprecate their own or show
Their pleasure at another's work,
They offer and accept their gifts,
Then sit to contemplate
The language of the rounded shape,
The grammar of its line, the vowels
Of glaze in phrase of craquelure,
So that the tacit meaning acts
Upon their minds,
Contracts to specks of black,
Collapsars that engulf all seeing
In eating up the space around,
Or hints in sheaves of light
At nebulae beyond the glimpse
Of other shapes they half-suggest,
A range of mountain tops
Or branches hooped with weight of snow.

WILLIAM ANDERSON

The Good Painter

The good painter:
the artist of the black and red ink of wisdom,
the creator of things with the black water . . .

this good painter, understanding,
with god in his heart,
who divines things with his heart,
holds a dialogue with his own heart.

He knows the colours, he applies them, he shades them.
He draws feet and faces,
traces the shadows, brings his work to perfection.
Like an artist
he paints the colours of all the flowers.

ANONYMOUS NAHUATL POEM
Translated from a Spanish version by J.M. Cohen

Morning

To find the Western path,
Right thro' the Gates of Wrath
I urge my way;
Sweet Mercy leads me on
With soft repentant moan:
I see the break of day.

The war of swords and spears,
Melted by dewy tears,
Exhales on high;
The Sun is freed from fears,
And with soft grateful tears
Ascends the sky.

WILLIAM BLAKE

The Cold Heaven

Suddenly I saw the cold and rook-delighting heaven
That seemed as though ice burned and was but the more ice,
And thereupon imagination and heart were driven
So wild that every casual thought of that and this

Vanished, and left but memories, that should be out of season
With the hot blood of youth, of love crossed long ago;
And I took all the blame out of all sense and reason,
Until I cried and trembled and rocked to and fro,
Riddled with light. Ah! when the ghost begins to quicken,
Confusion of the death-bed over, is it sent
Out naked on the roads, as the books say, and stricken
By the injustice of the skies for punishment?

W. B. YEATS

The Skaters

And in the frosty season, when the sun
Was set, and visible for many a mile
The cottage windows blazed through twilight gloom,
I heeded not their summons: happy time
It was indeed for all of us – for me
It was a time of rapture! Clear and loud
The village clock tolled six, – I wheeled about,
Proud and exulting like an untired horse
That cares not for his home. All shod with steel,
We hissed along the polished ice in games
Confederate, imitative of the chase
And woodland pleasures, – the resounding horn,
The pack loud chiming, and the hunted hare.
So through the darkness and the cold we flew,
And not a voice was idle; with the din
Smitten, the precipices rang aloud;
The leafless trees and every icy crag
Tinkled like iron; while far distant hills
Into the tumult sent an alien sound
Of melancholy not unnoticed, while the stars
Eastward were sparkling clear, and in the west
The orange sky of evening died away.

Not seldom from the uproar I retired
Into a silent bay, or sportively
Glanced sideway, leaving the tumultuous throng,
To cut across the reflex of a star
That fled, and, flying still before me, gleamed
Upon the glassy plain; and oftentimes,
When we had given our bodies to the wind,
And all the shadowy banks on either side
Came sweeping through the darkness, spinning still
The rapid line of motion, then at once
Have I, reclining back upon my heels,
Stopped short; yet still the solitary cliffs
Wheeled by me – even as if the earth had rolled
With visible motion her diurnal round!
Behind me did they stretch in solemn train,
Feebler and feebler, and I stood and watched
Till all was tranquil as a dreamless sleep.

WILLIAM WORDSWORTH
The Prelude, I. 425–63

The Valley Wind

Living in retirement beyond the World,
Silently enjoying isolation,
I pull the rope of my door tighter
And bind firmly this cracked jar.
My spirit is tuned to the Spring-season;
At the fall of the year there is autumn in my heart
Thus imitating cosmic changes
My cottage becomes a Universe.

LU-YÜN
Translated from the Chinese by Arthur Waley

From In Memoriam

To-night the winds begin to rise
    And roar from yonder dropping day:
    The last red leaf is whirl'd away,
The rooks are blown about the skies;

The forest crack'd, the waters curl'd,
    The cattle huddled on the lea;
    And wildly dash'd on tower and tree
The sunbeam strikes along the world:

And but for fancies, which aver
    That all thy motions gently pass
    Athwart a plane of molten glass,
I scarce could brook the strain and stir

That makes the barren branches loud;
    And but for fear it is not so,
    The wild unrest that lives in woe
Would dote and pore on yonder cloud

That rises upward always higher,
    And onward drags labouring breast,
    And topples round the dreary west,
A looming bastion fringed with fire.

ALFRED, LORD TENNYSON

On the Beach at Night Alone

On the beach at night alone,
As the old mother sways her to and fro singing her husky
    song,
As I watch the bright stars shining, I think a thought of the
    clef of the universes and of the future.
A vast similitude interlocks all,

All spheres, grown, ungrown, small, large, suns, moons,
  planets,
All distances of place however wide,
All distances of time, all inanimate forms,
All souls, all living bodies though they be ever so different, or
  in different worlds,
All gaseous, watery, vegetable, mineral processes, the fishes,
  the brutes,
All nations, colors, barbarisms, civilizations, languages,
All identities that have existed or may exist on this globe, or
  any globe,
All lives and deaths, all of the past, present, future,
This vast similitude spans them, and always has spann'd,
And shall forever span them and compactly hold and enclose
  them.

WALT WHITMAN

St Sophia: Sestina

This is a building to listen to; wisdom
Fills it with ghost choirs greeting the Emperor
And voices that answer from galleries of marble,
So vast in its volume of air that time
Preserves in the molecules all patterns of light,
All humming of music that ever broke silence.

Startled at being here, at seeing in silence
The dome that ballooned in the legends of wisdom,
I trust to my touch, not eyes or the light,
Finger the monogram of the dead Emperor,
Stroke columns where sunlight on fossilized time
Finds undersea forests in Armorican marble.

Christ the vine is alive in the marble
Of capitals grown in a forest of silence.
It is He who shaped it by entering time:
A model of mind that, echoing His wisdom,
Shows man the hemispheres of which He is Emperor,
The world-forming brain He makes conscious of light.

The sacred dances of the court catch light,
Their white robes gleam upon pavements of marble
Like reflection of doves round the blood-purple Emperor,
And happy with tears, without this silence,
I never could have guessed mind under wisdom
Veined out so hugely in branches of time.

Space of this order changes life in time:
The mosaic saints burn in the light;
Their sins are smelted to gold by wisdom
Whose greatest miracle, to raise stone, brick and marble
Was to call to its service, to abase with silence
His brothel-reared wife and the demon Emperor.

Crowds round the dome gaze at the Emperor,
Here made Christ's image to mankind in his time,
Where the seraphim pour on him vials of silence
And the eyes of the Virgin in the apse shine with light,
Melting to a mother the Empress of marble
In the church drawn to heaven by the gold chain of wisdom.

We are changed like the Emperor, charged now by wisdom
To speak in our time of the mercies of silence
Our words born of light, fit for minds cool as marble.

WILLIAM ANDERSON

PART FOUR
Your Place Is Lofty

To Viracocha

O Viracocha, Lord of the Universe,
be now man,
be now woman,
Lord of reproduction,
be now what you were,
O Lord of Divination!
where are you hiding now?
Now you are above,
now you are below,
or perhaps behind
your splendid throne and sceptre.
Oh, hear me!
In the tall skies
where maybe you dwell
or in the depths of the sea,
which may be your home,
creator of the world,
maker of humankind,
Lord of Lords,
my eyes are weak,
yet I long to see you,
my sole desire is to know you.
Were I but allowed to see you,
were I but allowed to know you,
were I but allowed to meditate on you
and to understand you!
Oh, deign to look on me,
for you know me!
Sun and moon,
day and night,
spring and winter,
not in vain did you ordain them.
O Viracocha,
they all recur
on the road you taught them,
they all arrive
at the goal you set them,
the point you willed for them.

You bear
your royal sceptre.
Oh, hear me!
Oh, pick me out!
Do not let me
grow weary
and die!

Anonymous Quechua hymn
Translated from a Spanish version by J. M. Cohen

Never Weather-Beaten Sail

Never weather-beaten sail more willing bent to shore,
   Never tired pilgrim's limbs affected slumber more,
Than my weary spright now longs to fly out of my troubled
      breast.
   O! come quickly, sweetest Lord, and take my soul to rest.

Ever blooming are the joys of Heaven's high Paradise.
   Cold age deafs not there our ears, nor vapour dims our eyes;
Glory there the sun outshines, whose beams the blessed only see.
   O! come quickly, glorious Lord, and raise my spright to thee.

Thomas Campion

Joy and Peace in Believing

Sometimes a light surprises
   The Christian while he sings;
It is the Lord who rises
   With healing in his wings:
When comforts are declining,
   He grants the soul again

74

A season of clear shining,
  To cheer it after rain.

In holy contemplation,
  We sweetly then pursue
The theme of God's salvation,
  And find it ever new.
Set free from present sorrow,
  We cheerfully can say,
E'en let th' unknown to-morrow
  Bring with it what it may!

It can bring with it nothing,
  But He will bear us through;
Who gives the lilies clothing,
  Will clothe his people too:
Beneath the spreading heavens
  No creature but is fed;
And He who feeds the ravens,
  Will give his children bread.

Though vine nor fig-tree neither
  Their wonted fruit should bear,
Though all the fields should wither,
  Nor flocks nor herds be there:
Yet God the same abiding,
  His praise shall tune my voice;
For, while in him confiding,
  I cannot but rejoice.

WILLIAM COWPER
Olney Hymns, no. XLVIII

Sunday

Sunday wears a crown, and has a golden beard and a ring.
Sunday sings his psalms, and laughs and jokes, and teaches his lessons in
    a booming voice.
And all creatures sleep in the peace of the earth, and the earth in
    Sunday's hand.

ELISEO DIEGO
Translated from the Spanish by J. M. Cohen

The Face of God

Lovely face, majestic face, face of beauty, face of
flame, the face of the Lord God of Israel when He sits
upon His throne of glory, robed in praise upon His seat
of splendour. His beauty surpasses the beauty of the
aged, His splendour outshines the splendour of newly-weds
in their bridal chamber.

Whoever looks at Him is instantly torn; whoever glimpses
His beauty immediately melts away. Those who serve Him
today no longer serve Him tomorrow; those who serve Him
tomorrow no longer serve Him afterwards; for their
strength fails and their faces are charred, their hearts
reel and their eyes grow dim at the splendour and
radiance of their king's beauty.

Beloved servants, lovely servants, swift servants, light-
footed servants, who stand before the stone of the throne
of glory, who wait upon the wheel of the chariot. When
the sapphire of the throne of glory whirls at them, when
the wheel of the chariot hurls past them, those on the
right now stand again to the left, those on the left now
stand again to the right, those in front now stand again
in back, those in back now stand again in front.

He who sees the one says, 'That is the other.' And he who
sees the other says, 'That is the one.' For the visage of
the one is like the visage of the other; and the visage
of the other is like the visage of the one.

Happy the King who has such servants, and happy the servants
who have such a King. Happy the eye that sees and feeds
upon this wondrous light – a wondrous vision and most strange!

HEKHALOT HYMN
Translated from the Hebrew by T. Carmi

Sophoclean Chorus

What man is he that yearneth
   For length unmeasured of days?
Folly mine eye discerneth
   Encompassing all his ways.
For years over-running the measure
   Shall change thee in evil wise
Grief draweth nigh thee; and pleasure,
   Behold, it is hid from thine eyes.
This to their wage have they
   Which overlive their day.
And He that looseth from labour
   Doth one with other befriend,
   Whom bride and bridegroom attend,
Song nor sound of the tabor,
   Death, that maketh an end.

Thy portion esteem I highest,
   Who wast not ever begot;
Thine next, being born who diest
   And straightway again art not.

With follies light as the feather
  Doth Youth to man befall;
Then evils gather together,
  There wants not one of them all –
  Wrath, envy, discord, strife,
  The sword that seeketh life.
And sealing the sum of trouble
  Doth tottering Age draw nigh,
  Whom friends and kinsfolk fly,
Age, upon whom redouble
  All sorrows under the sky.

This man, as me, even so
  Have the evil days overtaken,
And like as a cape sea-shaken
  With tempest at earth's last verges
And shock of all winds that blow,
  His head the seas of woe.
  The thunders of awful surges
Running overflow;
  Blown from the fall of even,
  Blown from the dayspring forth,
Blown from the noon in heaven,
  Blown from night and the North.

SOPHOCLES
Oedipus at Colonus, 121–48. Translated from the Greek by A. E.
Housman

Psalm 139

O Lord, thou hast searched me, and known me.

Thou knowest my downsitting and mine uprising, thou understandest my thought afar off.

Thou compassest my path and my lying down, and art acquainted with all my ways.

For there is not a word in my tongue, but, lo, O Lord, thou knowest it altogether.

Thou hast beset me behind and before, and laid thine hand upon me.

Such knowledge is too wonderful for me; it is high, I cannot attain unto it.

Whither shall I go from thy spirit? or wither shall I flee from thy presence?

If I ascend up into heaven, thou art there: if I make my bed in hell, behold, thou art there.

If I take the wings of the morning, and dwell in the uttermost parts of the sea;

Even there shall thy hand lead me, and thy right hand shall hold me.

If I say, Surely the darkness shall cover me; even the night shall be light about me.

Yea, the darkness hideth not from thee: but the night shineth as the day: the darkness and the light are both alike to thee.

For thou hast possessed my reins: thou hast covered me in my mother's womb.

I will praise thee; for I am fearfully and wonderfully made: marvellous are thy works; and that my soul knoweth right well.

My substance was not hid from thee, when I was made in secret, and curiously wrought in the lowest parts of the earth.

Thine eyes did see my substance, yet being unperfect; and in thy book all my members were written, which in continuance were fashioned, when as yet there was none of them.

How precious also are thy thoughts unto me, O God! how great is the sum of them!

If I should count them, they are more in number than the sand: when I awake, I am still with thee.

Lord, Where Shall I Find You?

Lord, where shall I find You? Your place is lofty and secret.
And where shall I not find you? The whole earth is full of
Your glory!

You are found in man's innermost heart, yet You fixed earth's
boundaries. You are a strong tower for those who are near,
and the trust of those who are far. You are enthroned on
the cherubim, yet You dwell in the heights of heaven. You
are praised by Your hosts, but even their praise is not worthy
of You. The sphere of heaven cannot contain You; how much
less the chambers of the Temple!

Even when You rise above Your hosts on a throne, high and
exalted, You are nearer to them than their own bodies and
souls. Their mouths attest that they have no Maker except
You. Who shall not fear You? All bear the yoke of Your
kingdom. And who shall not call to You? It is You who
give them their food.

I have sought to come near You, I have called to You with
all my heart; and when I went out towards You, I found
You coming towards me. I look upon Your wondrous power
with awe. Who can say that he has not seen You? The
heavens and their legions proclaim Your dread – without
a sound.

But can God really dwell among men? Their foundations are
dust – what can they conceive of Him? Yet You, O Holy One,
make Your home where they sing Your praises and Your glory.
The living creatures, standing on the summit of the world,
praise Your wonders. Your throne is above their heads, yet
it is You who carry them all!

JUDAH HALEVI
Translated from the Hebrew by T. Carmi

Milton in Old Age

Since I believe in God the Father Almighty,
Man's Maker and Judge, Overruler of Fortune,
'Twere strange should I praise anything and refuse Him praise,
Should love the creature forgetting the Creator,
Nor unto Him in suff'ring and sorrow turn me:
Nay how coud I withdraw me from His embracing?

But since that I have seen not, and cannot know Him,
Nor in my earthly temple apprehend rightly
His wisdom and the heav'nly purpose eternal;
Therefore will I be bound to no studied system
Nor argument, nor with delusion enslave me,
Nor seek to please Him in any foolish invention,
Which my spirit within me, that loveth beauty
And hateth evil, hath reprov'd as unworthy:

But I cherish my freedom in loving service,
Gratefully adoring for delight beyond asking
Or thinking, and in hours of anguish and darkness
Confiding always on His excellent greatness.

ROBERT BRIDGES

Hymn of the Nativity – Full Chorus

Wellcome, all WONDERS in one sight!
Aeternity shut in a span.
Sommer in Winter. Day in Night.
Heaven in earth, and GOD in MAN.
Great little one! whose all-embracing birth
Lifts earth to heaven, stoopes heav'n to earth.

WELLCOME. Though nor to gold nor silk,
To more than Caesar's birth right is;
　　Two sister-seas of Virgin-Milk,
With many a rarely-temper'd kisse
　　That breathes at once both MAID and MOTHER,
Warmes in the one, cooles in the other.

　　WELLCOME, though not to those gay flyes
Gilded ith' Beames of earthly kings;
　　Slippery soules in smiling eyes;
But to poor Shepherds, home-spun things:
　　Whose Wealth's their flock; whose wit, to be
Well read in their simplicity.

　　Yet when young April's husband showrs
Shall blesse the fruitfull Maia's bed,
　　We'll bring the First-born of her flowrs
To kisse thy FEET and crown thy HEAD.
　　To thee, dread Lamb! whose love must keep
The shepheards, more than they the sheep.

　　TO THEE, meek Majesty! soft KING
Of simple GRACES and sweet LOVES.
　　Each of us his lamb will bring
Each his pair of sylver Doves;
　　Till burnt at last in fire of Thy fair eyes,
Our selves become our own best SACRIFICE.

RICHARD CRASHAW

Peace After a Storm

When darkness long has veil'd my mind,
  And smiling day once more appears;
Then, my Redeemer, then I find
  The folly of my doubts and fears.

Straight I upbraid my wandering heart,
  And blush that I should ever be
Thus prone to act so base a part,
  Or harbour one hard thought of Thee!

Oh! let me then at length be taught
  What I am still so slow to learn;
That God is Love, and changes not,
  Nor knows the shadow of a turn.

Sweet truth, and easy to repeat!
  But, when my faith is sharply tried,
I find myself a learner yet,
  Unskilful, weak, and apt to slide.

But, O my Lord, one look from Thee
  Subdues the disobedient will;
Drives doubt and discontent away,
  And thy rebellious worm is still.

Thou art as ready to forgive
  As I am ready to repine;
Thou, therefore, all the praise receive;
  Be shame and self-abhorrence mine.

WILLIAM COWPER
Olney Hymns, no. XL

Pleasure It Is

Pleasure it is
To hear, iwis,
   The birdés sing.
The deer in the dale,
The sheep in the vale,
   The corn springing;
God's purveyance
For sustenance
   It is for man.
Then we always
To him give praise,
   And thank him than,
   And thank him than.

William Cornish

Affliction

When first thou didst entice to thee my heart,
         I thought the service brave:
So many joyes I writ down for my part,
         Besides what I might have
Out of my stock of naturall delights,
Augmented with thy gracious benefits.

I looked on thy furniture so fine,
         And made it fine to me:
Thy glorious houshold-stuffe did me entwine,
         And 'tice me unto thee.
Such starres I counted mine: both heav'n and earth
Payd me my wages in a world of mirth.

What pleasures could I want, whose King I served,
         Where joyes my fellows were?
Thus argu'd into hopes, my thoughts reserved
         No place for grief or fear.

Therefore my sudden soul caught at the place,
And made her youth and fierceness seek thy face.

At first thou gav'st me milk and sweetness;
        I had my wish and way:
My dayes were straw'd with flow'rs and happiness;
        There was no moneth but May.
But with my yeares sorrow did twist and grow,
And made a partie unawares for wo.

My flesh began unto my soul in pain,
        Sicknesses cleave my bones;
Consuming agues dwell in ev'ry vein,
        And tune my breath to grones.
Sorrow was all my soul; I scarce beleeved,
Till grief did tell me roundly, that I lived.

When I got health, thou took'st away my life,
        And more; for my friends die:
My mirth and edge was lost; a blunted knife
        Was of more use then I.
Thus thinne and lean without a fence or friend,
I was blown through with ev'ry storm and winde.

Whereas my birth and spirit rather took
        The way that takes the town;
Thou didst betray me to a lingring book,
        And wrap me in a gown.
I was entangled in the world of strife,
Before I had the power to change my life.

Yet, for I threatned oft the siege to raise,
        Not simpring all mine age,
Thou often didst with Academick praise
        Melt and dissolve my rage.
I took thy sweetned pill, till I came where
I could not go away, nor persevere.

Yet lest perchance I should too happie be
        In my unhappinesse,
Turning my purge to food, thou throwest me
        Into more sicknesses.
Thus doth thy power crosse-bias me, not making
Thine own gift good, yet me from my wayes taking.

Now I am here, what thou wilt do with me
        None of my books will show:
I reade, and sigh, and wish I were a tree;
        For sure then I should grow
To fruit or shade: at least some bird would trust
Her houshold to me, and I should be just.

Yet, though thou troublest me, I must be meek;
        In weaknesse must be stout.
Well, I will change the service, and go seek
        Some other master out.
Ah my deare God! though I am clean forgot,
Let me not love thee, if I love thee not.

GEORGE HERBERT

O Lamb of God

The Divine Vision still was seen
Still was the Human Form, Divine
    Weeping in weak and mortal clay
O Jesus still the Form was thine.

And thine the Human Face and thine
The Human Hands and Feet and Breath
    Entering thro' the Gates of Birth
And passing thro' the Gates of Death.

And O thou Lamb of God, whom I
Slew in my dark self-righteous pride:
    Art thou return'd to Albions Land!
And is Jerusalem thy Bride?

    Come to my arms and never more
Depart; but dwell for ever here;
    Create my Spirit to thy Love:
Subdue my Spectre to thy Fear.

WILLIAM BLAKE
From *Jerusalem* (Chapter 1, Plate 27, lines 57–73)

For Thine Own Sake, O My God

Wearied of sinning, wearied of repentance,
    Wearied of self, I turn, my God, to Thee;
To Thee, my Judge, on Whose all-righteous sentence
    Hangs mine eternity:
I turn to Thee, I plead Thyself with Thee, –
    Be pitiful to me.

Wearied I loathe myself, I loathe my sinning,
    My stains, my festering sores, my misery:
Thou the Beginning, Thou ere my beginning
    Didst see and didst foresee
Me miserable, me sinful, ruined me, –
    I plead Thyself with Thee.

I plead Thyself with Thee Who art my Maker,
    Regard Thy handiwork that cries to Thee;
I plead Thyself with Thee Who wast partaker
    Of mine infirmity;
Love made Thee what Thou art, the love of me, –
    I plead Thyself with Thee.

CHRISTINA ROSSETTI

Obeisance to the Guru

'Obeisance to the Body of my Lord, the *Guru*!
O grant that I may cling successfully to solitude.

'My happiness unknown unto my relatives,
My sorrowing unknown unto mine enemies –
Could thus I die, amid this Solitude,
Contented would I be, I the devotee.

'My growing old unknown unto my betrothed,
My falling ill unknown unto my sister –
Could thus I die, amid this Solitude,
Contented would I be, I the devotee.

'My death unknown to any human being,
My rotting corpse unseen by birds –
Could thus I die, amid this Solitude,
Contented would I be, I the devotee.

'My putrid flesh sucked by the flies,
My dissolving muscles eaten by the worms –
Could thus I die, amid this Solitude,
Contented would I be, I the devotee.

'With no human foot-print by my door,
With no mark of blood within (the Cave) –
Could thus I die, amid this Solitude,
Contented would I be, I the devotee.

'With none to crowd about my corpse (or bier),
With none to lament o'er my death –
Could thus I die, amid this Solitude,
Contented would I be, I the devotee.

'With none to ask where I had gone,
And with no place which one might point to as my goal –
Could thus I die, amid this Solitude,
Contented would I be, I the devotee.

'Thus, may this prayer about the manner of my death
Amid this uninhabited Solitude
Bear fruit, and, for all beings good, be granted as I wish;
Then satisfied I'll die, I the devotee.'

MILAREPA
Translated from the Tibetan by W. Y. Evans-Wentz

An Holy Sonnet to the Precious Blood of Christ

Victorious Monarchs are of right array'd
In crimson Surcoat. This all glorious King,
Of right by mocking souldiers is display'd
In princelie Robe that marks his Triumphing.
O Purple, of thy precious tincture bring
Myriad empurpled Teares, to fill my head,
That on thy sacred Mysterie pondering,
Mine eyes upon these Hymns bloud-gouts may shed.
Thy bloudie Hue oure sinnes doth signifie
Which on the Lambe the Father will'd should lie;
Christ to this load hath bowed his Backe submiss.
O Christ, O blessed Lambe, vouchsafe to mee
To enfold my scarlet sinnes, sprung from the Abyss,
In the bloud-stained Robe of thy Humanitie.

JEAN DE LA CEPPÈDE
Translated from the French by 'Alberick'

Lachrimae Verae

Crucified Lord, you swim upon your cross
and never move. Sometimes in dreams of hell
the body moves but moves to no avail
and is at one with that eternal loss.

You are the castaway of drowned remorse,
you are the world's atonement on the hill.
This is your body twisted by our skill
into a patience proper for redress.

I cannot turn aside from what I do;
you cannot turn away from what I am.
You do not dwell in me nor I in you

however much I pander to your name
or answer to your lords of revenue,
surrendering the joys that they condemn.

GEOFFREY HILL

The Church Windows

Lord, how can man preach thy eternall word?
    He is a brittle crazie glasse:
Yet in thy temple thou dost him afford
    This glorious and transcendent place,
    To be a window, through thy grace.

But when thou dost anneal in glasse thy storie,
    Making thy life to shine within
The holy Preachers; then the light and glorie
    More rev'rend grows, and more doth win;
    Which else shows watrish, bleak, and thin.

Doctrine and life, colours and light, in one
    When they combine and mingle, bring
A strong regard and aw: but speech alone
    Doth vanish like a flaring thing,
    And in the eare, not conscience ring.

GEORGE HERBERT

90

The Garden

Again the garden has got the glitter of Spring:
The nightingale hears good news, for the rose is come.

Soft wind returning to the young plants of the meadow,
Greet for us the rose, the cypress and the sweet basil.

They are spread for the wedding-feast of the wine-seller's son,
And I'd sweep his floor with my eyelashes to win such grace.

For that amber-scented strand you draw across a moonlight brow
Has made a shuttlecock of my heart, and set it spinning.

I can't trust those who sneer at us drinking down to the lees:
That is the kind of thing which gets a bad name for religion.

Let them learn to be friends with God's true friends; remember that
      Noah in his ark,
A speck of dust himself, cared not a drop for the deluge.

Go out through the door of the house of Fate with its shifting spheres,
Nor drink of the sky's black bowl – it kills its guest at the last.

Tell those whose holding at length is no more than a fistful of dust:
'What need of these proud domes you rear to the sky?'

But as for you, you are Joseph, you are the Moon of Canaan:
The stewardship of Egypt is yours; so bid this prison good-bye.

Hafiz, drink wine, and be glad and reckless; but don't copy those
Who make reciting the Book a cover for lies.

HAFIZ
Translated from the Persian by Peter Avery and John Heath-Stubbs

I Live with Him

I live with Him – I see His face –
I go no more away
For Visitor – or Sundown –
Death's single privacy

The Only One – forestalling Mine –
And that – by Right that He
Presents a Claim invisible –
No wedlock – granted Me –

I live with Him – I hear His Voice –
I stand alive – Today –
To witness to the Certainty
Of Immortality –

Taught Me – by Time – the lower Way –
Conviction – Every day –
That Life like This – is stopless –
Be Judgment – what it may –

EMILY DICKINSON

Nothing There but Faith

Nothing, it seemed, between them and the grave.
No, as I looked, there was nothing anywhere.
You'd think no ground could be so flat and bare:
No little ridge or hump or bush to brave
The horizon. Yet they called that land their land,
Without a single thought drank in that air
As simple and equivocal as despair.
This, this was what I could not understand.

92

The reason was, there was nothing there but faith.
Faith made the whole, yes all they could see or hear
Or touch or think, and arched its break of day
Within them and around them every way.
They looked: all was transfigured far and near,
And the great world rolled between them and death.

EDWIN MUIR

At a Mass

Waiting restlessly the coming event,
Hearing the three bells ringing the loud warning,
I look for the lifted moment, the lifted cup,
Feeling upon my skin the Roman morning.
I watch with a critical eye the bread raised up
And confuse aesthetics now with a sacrament.

It is the veils drawn over, the decent hiding
That recall the decorum the test of art demands.
Around me the people pray, forgetful of
Even their painful eyes, their well-worn hands.
I struggle now with my own ideas of love
And wonder if art and religion mean dividing.

Each has his way and mine perhaps is to
Suffer the critical sense that cannot rest.
If the air is cool, the colours right, the spoken
Words dramatic enough, then I am pleased.
But why must I ask a sense of style in the broken
Bread and bring God down to my limited view?

Pride enfolds me, pride in the gift of tongues;
Envy too, since I long to be like these
Who approach with empty hands, an open heart –
The simple men lost in simplicities.
I have to endure the ecstatic pain of art
And shape from the silence all my encroaching songs.

ELIZABETH JENNINGS

Magic Strings

The witch pours the libation, clouds fill the sky,
In the flaming coals of the jade brazier the fumes of incense
    throb.
The God of the Sea and the Hill Nymph take their places,
Votive papers rustle in the howling whirlwind.
On her inlaid lute of passion-wood a goldleaf phoenix dances:
With knitted brow at each muttered phrase she plucks the
    strings once.
She calls to the stars and summons the demons to taste of her
    dish and cup:
Mankind shudders when the mountain goblins feed.
The glow of the sun behind Chung-nan hangs low in a trough
    of the hills:
The gods are here, for ever present between somewhere and
    nowhere!
The gods scold, the gods are pleased, in spasms on the
    medium's face.
 – Then the gods with a myriad outriders go back to the blue
    mountains.

LI-HO
Translated from the Chinese by A. C. Graham

94

Teresa's Vocation*

Away from this world,
contemplating the snowy hills,
beyond which she imagined God,
(for beyond them she could see nothing but sky).
More than ever she desired life
and the wonder of knowing herself neither deaf nor blind.
With a loving cry he had begged her
to return
and feel the wind on her face,
and become aware of his kiss on her hands.
But there is no triumph in her heart.
God is everywhere, her master,
her impresario,
her husband,
her son,
her lover,
her lucky charm.
There is no triumph in her heart.
All women belong to God
and He belongs to none of them.
Evening after evening she sees the hills rise up,
pyramids on which the snow makes its nest.
She thinks of other women,
poor provincial girls
with a vocation for the hearth,
sometimes visited by the Devil,
and abandoned among the dry leaves
that fall from the shadowy trees.

BELKIS CUZA MALÉ
Translated from the Spanish by J. M. Cohen

*Teresa is Teresa de Cepeda of Ávila, who became Santa Teresa de Jesús

Teresa of Avila

Spain, The wild dust, the whipped corn, earth easy for
footsteps, shallow to starving seeds. High sky at night
like walls. Silences surrounding Avila.

She, teased by questions, aching for reassurance. Calm
in confession before incredulous priests. Then back – to
the pure illumination, the profound personal prayer,
the four waters.

Water from the well first, drawn up painfully. Clinking
of pails. Dry lips at the well-head. Parched grass bending.
And the dry heart too – waiting for prayer.

Then the water-wheel, turning smoothly. Somebody
helping unseen. A keen hand put out, gently sliding
the wheel. Then water and the aghast spirit refreshed
and quenched.

Not this only. Other waters also, clear from a spring or a
pool. Pouring from a fountain like child's play – but the
child is elsewhere. And see, kneeling, cooling her
spirit at the water, comes nearer, nearer.

Then the entire cleansing, utterly from nowhere. No
wind ruffled it, no shadows slid across it. Her mind
met it, her will approved. And all beyonds, backwaters,
dry words of old prayers were lost in it. The water
was only itself.

And she knelt there, waited for shadows to cross the
light which the water made, waited for familiar
childhood illuminations (the lamp by the bed, the
candle in church, sun beckoned by horizons) – but this
light was none of these, was only how the water looked,
how the will turned and was still. Even the image of
light itself withdrew, and the dry dust on the winds of

Spain outside her halted. Moments spread not into
hours but stood still. No dove brought the tokens of
peace. She was the peace that her prayer had promised.
And the silences suffered no shadows.

ELIZABETH JENNINGS

From A Song to David

Glorious the sun in mid career;
Glorious th' assembled fires appear;
   Glorious the comet's train:
Glorious the trumpet and alarm;
Glorious th' almighty stretch'd-out arm;
   Glorious th' enraptur'd main:

Glorious the northern lights astream;
Glorious the song, when God's the theme
   Glorious the thunder's roar:
Glorious hosanna from the den;
Glorious the catholic amen;
   Glorious the martyr's gore:

Glorious – more glorious is the crown
Of Him that brought salvation down
   By meekness, call'd thy Son;
Thou that stupendous truth believ'd,
And now the matchless deed's achiev'd,
   Determined, Dared, and Done.

CHRISTOPHER SMART

He Fumbles at Your Soul

He fumbles at your Soul
As Players at the Keys
Before they drop full Music on –
He stuns you by degrees –
Prepares your brittle Nature
For the Ethereal Blow
By fainter Hammers – further heard –
Then nearer – Then so slow
Your Breath has time to straighten –
Your Brain – to bubble Cool –
Deals – One – imperial – Thunderbolt –
That scalps your naked Soul –

When Winds take Forests in their Paws –
The Universe – is still –

EMILY DICKINSON

From The Cherubic Wanderer

How marvellous that I, a dirty clod,
May yet hold friendly discourse with my God!

*

In hell itself there can your heaven be,
If, says the Lord, you give your soul to me.

*

Pleasing to God are all a good man's ways,
Equally when he drinks and when he prays.

ANGELUS SILESIUS
Translated from the German by J. M. Cohen

PART FIVE

Dust as We Are

Dust as We Are

Dust as we are, the immortal spirit grows
Like harmony in music; there is a dark
Inscrutable workmanship that reconciles
Discordant elements, makes them cling together
In one society. How strange that all
The terrors, pains, and early miseries,
Regrets, vexations, lassitudes interfused
Within my mind, should e'er have borne a part,
And that a needful part, in making up
The calm existence that is mine when I
Am worthy of myself! Praise to the end!
Thanks to the means which Nature deigned to employ;
Whether her fearless visitings, or those
That came with soft alarm, like hurtless light
Opening the peaceful clouds; or she may use
Severer interventions, ministry
More palpable, as best might suit her aim.

WILLIAM WORDSWORTH
The Prelude, I. 340–56

Thou Who Didst Make

Thou Who didst make and knowest whereof we are made,
  Oh bear in mind our dust and nothingness,
  Our worldless tearless numbness of distress:
Bear Thou in mind the burden Thou hast laid
Upon us, and our feebleness unstayed
  Except Thou stay us: for the long long race
  Which stretches far and far before our face
Thou knowest, – remember Thou whereof we are made
If making makes us Thine then Thine we are,
  And if redemption we are twice Thine own:
If once Thou didst come down from heaven afar

101

To seek us and to find us, how not save?
  Comfort us, save us, leave us not alone,
Thou Who didst die our death and fill our grave.

CHRISTINA ROSSETTI

Psalm 131

Lord, my heart is not haughty, nor mine eyes lofty:
neither do I exercise myself in great matters, or in
things too high for me.
  Surely I have behaved and quieted myself, as a child
that is weaned of his mother: my soul is even as a weaned
child.
  Let Israel hope in the Lord from henceforth and for
ever.

Before I Was

Before I was, Your enduring love came to me, O You
who make being out of nothingness, and You created
me. Who was it that designed my form? Who cast
my body in a crucible and then made it congeal?
Who was it that breathed into me the breath of life?
Who opened the belly of Sheol and brought me forth?
Who has been my guide from boyhood to this day? Who
taught me wisdom and showed me wonders? Yes, I am
like clay in Your hands. Truly, it was You, not I,
that made me. And so I shall confess my guilt; nor
shall I say, 'It was the serpent who conspired to
deceive me.' How could I ever conceal my sin from
You? Even before I was, Your enduring love came to me!

SOLOMON IBN GABIROL
Translated from the Hebrew by T. Carmi

Truth of All Truth

Truth of all truth,
O Life, O Truth, O Way,
Who by the strait paths of thy Truth
Drivest our sin beyond the threshold of our door,
To thee, Incarnate Word,
Faith, Hope, and Charity
Continually do cry.

Thou who dost set thy prisoner at thy bar, and then
Makest him a man again,
And for that forespent carnal ecstasy,
Givest such grace,
That he accounts him blessed.
O miracle of strength!
O kingly word,
That once a sick man heard,
'Arise, take up thy bed, and go thy way.'

From the *Benedictbeuern* ms
Translated from the Latin by Helen Waddell

Christ's Bounties

. . . O Son of God, do a miracle for me, and change my
heart; Thy having taken flesh to redeem me was more
difficult than to transform my wickedness.

It is Thou who, to help me, didst go to be scourged by the
Jews; Thou, dear child of Mary, art the refined molten
metal of our forge.

It is Thou who makest the sun bright, together with the ice;
it is Thou who createdst the rivers and the salmon all along
the river.

That the nut-tree should be flowering, O Christ, it is a
rare craft; through Thy skill too comes the kernel, Thou
fair ear of our wheat.

Though the children of Eve ill deserve the bird-flocks and
the salmon, it was the Immortal One on the cross who
made both salmon and birds.

It is He who makes the flower of the sloes grow through
the surface of the blackthorn, and the nut-flower on other
trees; beside this, what miracle is greater?

ANONYMOUS
Translated from the Irish by Kenneth H. Jackson

Blessing
. . . the continual dew of Thy blessing . . .
(The Book of Common Prayer)

Not only for the small blind eyes of dew,
though ever-waking, nor the rainbow's promise,
although a giant image of those waters;
nor the uncovenanted lights that wash
dark and the day in spectre, though unbounded:
not thankfulness for these alone, by sight
or symbol; but for laws that gave us them.

All the great shining of so many mercies
impurely reaches us through prism and lens
of angel-flesh or blood-of-clouds or sky-dust:
blessing is mediate, screened by elements,
flying the lanes of sense, empowered by sense:
if light is pure it is invisible
(the dark of God); light is the eye that sees.

Blessing is mediate, even that of love:
our thicker flesh, our living dust, our white
and crimson distillations, are the world
by which it acts, unguessed without them; love
enthroned in secrecy, but love which is
a peacock wheel of stars, a moon, a morning,
a rainbow peace, and a continual dew.

TERENCE TILLER

Apologia

I read or write, I teach or wonder what is truth,
    I call upon my God by night and day.
I eat and freely drink, I make my rhymes,
    And snoring sleep, or vigil keep and pray.
And very ware of all my shames I am;
    O Mary, Christ, have mercy on your man.

SEDULIUS SCOTTUS
Translated from the Latin by Helen Waddell

From The Cherubic Wanderer

It's not the world, but you that are the world and bind
Yourself, within the prison of yourself confined.

ANGELUS SILESIUS
Translated from the German by J. M. Cohen

From To think of Time

What will be will be well, for what is is well,
To take interest is well, and not to take interest shall be well.

The domestic joys, the daily housework or business, the
  building of houses, are not phantasms, they have weight,
  form, location,
Farms, profits, crops, markets, wages, government, are none
  of them phantasms,
The difference between sin and goodness is no delusion,
The earth is not an echo, man and his life and all the things of
  his life are well-consider'd.

You are not thrown to the winds, you gather certainly and
  safely around yourself,
Yourself! yourself! yourself, for ever and ever!

WALT WHITMAN

Patience

Patience, better than armour, guards from harm.
And why seek enemies, if you have anger?
With friends, you need no medicine for danger.
With kinsmen, why ask fire to keep you warm?
What use are snakes when slander sharper stings?
What use is wealth where wisdom brings content?
With modesty, what need for ornament?
With poetry's Muse, why should we envy kings?

BHARTRHARI
Translated from the Sanskrit by John Brough

From Lucretius

The Gods, who haunt
The lucid interspace of world and world,
Where never creeps a cloud, or moves a wind,
Nor ever falls the least white star of snow,
Nor ever lowest roll of thunder moans,
Nor sound of human sorrow mounts to mar
Their sacred everlasting calm! and such,
Not all so fine, nor so divine a calm,
Not such, nor all unlike it, man may gain
Letting his own life go. The Gods, the Gods!
If all be atoms, how then should the Gods
Being atomic not be dissoluble,
Not follow the great law?

ALFRED, LORD TENNYSON

Wilt Thou Love God

Wilt thou love God, as he thee! then digest,
My Soule, this wholsome meditation,
How God the Spirit, by Angels waited on
In heaven, doth make his Temple in thy brest.
The Father having begot a Sonne most blest,
And still begetting, (for he ne'r begonne)
Hath deign'd to chuse thee by adoption,
Coheire to' his glory,' and Sabbaths endlesse rest;
And as a robb'd man, which by search doth finde
His stolne stuffe sold, must lose or buy' it againe:
The Sonne of glory came downe, and was slaine,
Us whom he' had made, and Satan stolne, to unbinde.
'Twas much, that man was made like God before,
But, that God should be made like man, much more.

JOHN DONNE

107

From Jubilate Agno

For I will consider my Cat Jeoffry.
For he is the servant of the Living God, duly and daily
    serving him.
For at the first glance of the glory of God in the East he
    worships in his way.
For is this done by wreathing his body seven times round with
    elegant quickness.
For then he leaps up to catch the musk, which is the blessing
    of God upon his prayer.
For he rolls upon prank to work it in.
For having done duty and received blessing he begins to consider
    himself.
For this he performs in ten degrees.
For first he looks upon his fore-paws to see if they are clean.
For secondly he kicks up behind to clear away there.

*   *   *

For thirdly he works it upon stretch with the fore-paws extended.
For fourthly he sharpens his paws by wood.
For fifthly he washes himself.
For sixthly he rolls upon wash.
For seventhly he fleas himself, that he may not be interrupted
    upon the beat.
For eighthly he rubs himself upon a post.
For ninthly he looks up for his instructions.
For tenthly he goes in quest of food.
For having consider'd God and himself he will consider his
    neighbour.
For if he meets another cat he will kiss her in kindness.
For when he takes his prey he plays with it to give it chance.
For one mouse in seven escapes by his dallying.
For when his day's work is done his business more properly begins.
For he keeps the Lord's watch in the night against the adversary.
For he counteracts the powers of darkness by his electrical skin
    and glaring eyes.
For he counteracts the Devil, who is death, by brisking about
    the life.
For in his morning orisons he loves the sun and the sun loves him.

For he is of the tribe of Tiger.

For the Cherub Cat is a term of the Angel Tiger.

For he has the subtlety and hissing of a serpent, which in
goodness he suppresses.

For he will not do destruction, if he is well-fed, neither
will he spit without provocation.

For he purrs in thankfulness, when God tells him he's a good Cat.

For he is an instrument for the children to learn benevolence
upon.

For every house is incomplete without him and a blessing is
lacking in the spirit.

For the Lord commanded Moses concerning the cats at the
departure of the Children of Israel from Egypt.

CHRISTOPHER SMART

Maelisu's Hymn to the Archangel Michael

O angel!
Bear, O Michael of great miracles,
To the Lord my plaint.

Hearest thou?
Ask of forgiving God
Forgiveness of all my vast evil.

Delay not!
Carry my fervent prayer
To the King, to the great King!

To my soul
Bring help, bring comfort
At the hour of its leaving earth.

Stoutly
To meet my expectant soul
Come with many thousand angels!

O soldier!
Against the crooked, wicked, militant world
Come to my help in earnest!

Do not
Disdain what I say!
As long as I live do not desert me!

Thee I choose,
That thou mayst save my soul,
My mind, my sense, my body.

O thou of goodly counsels,
Victorious, triumphant one,
Angelic slayer of Antichrist!

ANONYMOUS
Translated from the Irish by Kuno Meyer

The Wells of Jesus Wounds

Jesus woundes so wide
Ben* welles of lif to the goode,
Namely† the stronde‡ of his side,
That ran full breme§ on the Rode.

110

Yif thee liste to drinke,
To fle fro the fendes of helle,
Bowe thu down to the brinke,
And mekely taste of the welle.

ANONYMOUS

* *Ben*: are
† *Namely*: especially
‡ *stronde*: stream
§ *breme*: fiercely

His Litanie, to the Holy Spirit

In the houre of my distresse,
When temptations me oppresse,
And when I my sins confesse,
    Sweet Spirit comfort me!

When I lie within my bed,
Sick in heart, and sick in head,
And with doubts discomforted,
    Sweet Spirit comfort me!

When the house doth sigh and weep,
And the world is drown'd in sleep,
Yet mine eyes the watch do keep;
    Sweet Spirit comfort me!

When the artlesse Doctor sees
No one hope, but of his Fees,
And his skill runs on the lees;
    Sweet Spirit comfort me!

When his Potion and his Pill,
Has, or none, or little skill,
Meet for nothing, but to kill;
    Sweet Spirit comfort me!

When the passing-bell doth toll,
And the Furies in a shoal
Come to fright a parting soule;
    Sweet Spirit comfort me!

When the tapers now burne blew,
And the comforters are few,
And that number more than true;
    Sweet Spirit comfort me!

When the Priest his last hath pray'd,
And I nod to what is said,
'Cause my speech is now decay'd;
    Sweet Spirit comfort me!

When (God knowes) I'm tost about,
Either with despaire, or doubt;
Yet before the glasse be out,
    Sweet Spirit comfort me!

When the Tempter me pursu'th
With the sins of all my youth,
And halfe damns me with untruth;
    Sweet Spirit comfort me!

When the flames and hellish cries
Fright mine eares, and fright mine eyes,
And all terrors me surprize;
    Sweet Spirit comfort me!

When the Judgment is reveal'd,
And that open'd which was seal'd,
When to Thee I have appeal'd;
Sweet Spirit comfort me!

ROBERT HERRICK

Good Friday, 1613. Riding Westward

Let mans Soule be a Spheare, and then, in this,
The intelligence that moves, devotion is,
And as the other Spheares, by being growne
Subject to forraigne motions, lose their owne,
And being by others hurried every day,
Scarce in a yeare their naturall forme obey:
Pleasure or businesse, so, our Soules admit
For their first mover, and are whirld by it.
Hence is't, that I am carryed towards the West
This day, when my Soules forme bends toward the East.
There I should see a Sunne, by rising set,
And by that setting endlesse day beget;
But that Christ on this Crosse, did rise and fall,
Sinne had eternally benighted all.
Yet dare I'almost be glad, I do not see
That spectacle of too much weight for mee.
Who sees Gods face, that is selfe life, must dye;
What a death were it then to see God dye?
It made his owne Lieutenant Nature shrinke,
It made his footstoole crack, and the Sunne winke.
Could I behold those hands which span the Poles,
And tune all spheares at once, peirc'd with those holes?
Could I behold that endlesse height which is
Zenith to us, and our Antipodes,

Humbled below us? or that blood which is
The seat of all our Soules, if not of his,
Made durt of dust, or that flesh which was worne
By God, for his apparell, rag'd, and torne?
If on these things I durst not looke, durst I
Upon his miserable mother cast mine eye,
Who was Gods partner here, and furnish'd thus
Halfe of that Sacrifice, which ransom'd us?
Though these things, as I ride, be from mine eye,
They'are present yet unto my memory,
For that looks towards them; and thou look'st towards mee,
O Saviour, as thou hang'st upon the tree;
I turne my backe to thee, but to receive
Corrections, till thy mercies bid thee leave.
O thinke mee worth thine anger, punish mee,
Burne off my rusts, and my deformity,
Restore thine Image, so much, by thy grace,
That thou may'st know mee, and I'll turne my face.

JOHN DONNE

Prayer

Prayer the Churches banquet, Angels age,
   Gods breath in man returning to his birth,
The soul in paraphrase, heart in pilgrimage,
    The Christian plummet sounding heav'n and earth;

Engine against th' Almightie, sinners towre,
   Reversed thunder, Christ-side-piercing spear,
The six-daies-world-transposing in an houre,
    A kinde of tune, which all things heare and fear;

Softnesse, and peace, and joy, and love, and blisse,
  Exalted Manna, gladnesse of the best,
  Heaven in ordinarie, man well drest,
The milkie way, the bird of Paradise,

Church-bells beyond the starres heard, the souls blood,
The land of spices, something understood.

GEORGE HERBERT

Ex Nihilo

Here am I now cast down
Beneath the black glare of a netherworld's
Dead suns, dust in my mouth, among
Dun tiers no tears refresh: am cast
Down by a lofty hand,

Hand that I love! Lord Light,
How dark is Thy arm's will and ironlike
Thy ruler's finger that has sent me here!
Far from Thy Face I nothing understand,
But kiss the Hand that has consigned

Me to these latter years where I must learn
The revelation of despair, and find
Among the debris of all certainties
The hardest stone on which to found
Altar and shelter for Eternity.

DAVID GASCOYNE

Prayer

O my God do not part me from thee
Do not part me from thy sight

To love you is my faith and belief
Do not part my belief from my faith

I'm withered, become like the autumn
Do not part the leaves from the branch

My Master is a rose, I his leaf
Do not part the leaf from the rose

I, a nightingale in my love's garden
Do not part his beak from his song

All the fish breathe in water they say
Do not part the fish from the lake

Esrefoglu is thy humble slave
Do not part the Sultan from his servant.

EŞREFOĞLU
Translated from the Turkish by Taner Baybars

A Good-Night

Close now thine eyes, and rest secure;
    Thy *Soule* is safe enough; thy Body sure;
He that loves thee, he that keepes
And guards thee, never slumbers, never sleepes.
The smiling Conscience in a sleeping breast
    Has only peace, has only rest:
    The musicke and the mirth of Kings,
Are all but very *Discords*, when she sings:
    Then close thine Eyes and rest secure;
No sleepe so sweet as thine, no rest so sure.

FRANCIS QUARLES

Hymn

'To the impure eyes of them Thou seekest to liberate,
Thou manifestest Thyself in a variety of shapes;
But to those of Thy followers who have been purified,
Thou, Lord, appearest as a Perfected Being; obeisance to Thee.

'With Thy Brahma-like voice, endowed with the sixty vocal
        perfections,
Thou preachest the Holy Truths to each in his own speech,
Complete in their eighty-four thousand subjects;
Obeisance to Thy Word, audible yet inseparable from the Voidness.

'In the Heavenly Radiance of *Dharma-Kaya* Mind,
There existeth not shadow of thing or concept,
Yet It prevadeth all objects of knowledge;
Obeisance to the Immutable, Eternal Mind.

'In the Holy Palace of the Pure and Spiritual Realms,
Thou Person illusory, yet changeless and selfless,
Thou Mother Divine of Buddhas, past, present, and future,
O Great Mother Damema, to Thy Feet I bow down.

117

'(O *Guru*), to Thy children spiritual,
To Thy disciples who Thy word obey,
To each, with all his followers,
Obeisance humble and sincere I make.

'Whate'er there be, in all the systems of the many worlds,
To serve as offerings for the rites divine,
I offer unto Thee, along with mine own fleshly form;
Of all my sins, may I be freed and purified.

'In merits earned by others, I rejoice;
So set the Wheel of Truth in motion full, I pray;
Until the Whirling Pool of Being emptied be,
Do not, O Noble *Guru*, from the world depart.

'I dedicate all merit from this Hymn,
Unto the Cause of Universal Good.'

MILAREPA
Translated from the Tibetan by W. Y. Evans-Wentz

To Give the World for Nothing

to give the world for nothing is love
to let life flow away is love
offering the lump of sugar in your hand to another
swallowing the poison yourself is love
plagues falling from the sky like rain
holding up your head against them is love
this universe is a sea of fire
throwing yourself into it is love
you Esrefoglu of Anatolia know the truth
making the body mortal is love

EŞREFOĞLU
Translated from the Turkish by Murat Nemet-Nejat

The Soul and Its Maker

Bow down before God, my precious thinking soul,
and make haste to worship Him with reverence.
Night and day think only of your everlasting world.
Why should you chase after vanity and emptiness?
As long as you live, you are akin to the living God:
just as He is invisible, so are you. Since your
Creator is pure and flawless, know that you too are
pure and perfect. The Mighty One upholds the heavens
on His arm, as you uphold the mute body. My soul,
let your songs come before your Rock, who does not
lay your form in the dust. My innermost heart,
bless your Rock always, whose name is praised by
everything that has breath.

SOLOMON IBN GABIROL
Translated from the Hebrew by T. Carmi

The Pursuit of God

Grasp the Skirt of his Grace, for on a sudden He will flee away:
But draw Him not impatiently to thee, lest He fly as an arrow from the
    bow.
What shape will He not assume? What shifts He employeth!
If He be apprehended in Form, He will flee by way of the Spirit:
If thou seek Him in the sky, He will gleam in the water like the moon:
If thou go into the water, He fleeth to the sky:
If thou seek Him in the spaceless, He beckoneth to Space:
When thou seekest Him in Space, He fleeth to the spaceless. . . .
His Name will flee, the while thou mouldest thy lips for speech:
Thou may'st not even say, Such an one will flee:
He will flee from thee, so that if thou paint his picture,
The picture will flee from the tablet, and his features from thy soul.

RŪMĪ
Translated by Hasan Shahid Suhrawardy and revised by Robert Bridges

From The Book of Hours

Dear neighbour God, if often I disturb you
in the long nights with my hard knocking, I do so because
I seldom hear you breathing,
and I know that you are all alone in your great room,
and should you need something, there's no one there
to hold a drink out to your groping hand.
I'm always listening. Give me just a sign.
I am quite near.

There's only a thin wall between us,
by merest chance, and it would take
no more than a sound of your voice or of mine
to break it down.
Its fall would make no noise at all.
That wall is built of images of you.

Those pictures of you mask you like names,
and when for once the light in me flares up
by which I know you in my deepest self,
the light is squandered on mere picture-frames.

And then my senses, which grow quickly lame,
being severed from you, are without a home.

RAINER MARIA RILKE
Translated from the German by J. M. Cohen

The Friend

What pearl art Thou, that no man may pay thy price?
What doth the World offer, which is not a gift from Thee?
What punishment is greater, than to dwell afar from thy Face?
Torture not thy slave, tho' he be unworthy of Thee!

120

Whoever is whelm'd in the waves of Chance, can never escape, if he
    look not to Thee as Friend.
The World hath no permanence: what it hath I esteem as perishable, for
    it is strange to thy permanence. . . .
My wish ever is to fling my heart and my soul at thy Feet.
Dust be on the head of the soul, that hath received not the dust of thy
    Feet! . . .
I will not shun thy stroke: for impure is the heart that hath not burn'd
    in the flame of thine Affliction.
No end is there, O Lord, to thy praises, and no count of thy Praisers.
What atom is there that danceth not with abandon in thy praise?

Shams-I-Tabriz, beauty and pride of the skies, saith:
What king is there, but with heart and soul is a beggar of Thee?

RŪMĪ
Translated from the Persian by Hasan Shahid Suhrawardy and revised by Robert Bridges

The Kingdom of God

O world invisible, we view thee,
O world intangible, we touch thee,
O world unknowable, we know thee,
Inapprehensible, we clutch thee!

Does the fish soar to find the ocean,
The eagle plunge to find the air –
That we ask of the stars in motion
If they have rumour of thee there?

Not where the wheeling systems darken,
And our benumbed conceiving soars! –
The drift of pinions, would we harken,
Beats at our own clay-shuttered doors.

The angels keep their ancient places; –
Turn but a stone, and start a wing!
'Tis ye, 'tis your estrangèd faces,
That miss the many-splendoured thing.

But (when so sad thou canst not sadder)
Cry; – and upon thy so sore loss
Shall shine the traffic of Jacob's ladder
Pitched betwixt Heaven and Charing Cross.

Yea, in the night, my Soul, my daughter,
Cry, – clinging Heaven by the hems;
And lo, Christ walking on the water
Not of Gennesareth, but Thames!

FRANCIS THOMPSON

From A Song to David

For Adoration, in the skies,
The Lord's philosopher espies
　　The Dog, the Ram, and Rose;
The planets ring, Orion's Sword;
Nor is his greatness less ador'd
　　In the vile worm that glows.

For Adoration on the strings
The western breezes work their wings,
　　The captive ear to sooth. –
Hark! 'tis a voice – how still, and small –
That makes the cataracts to fall,
　　Or bids the sea be smooth.

For Adoration, incense comes
From bezoar, and Arabian gums;
   And on the civet's furr.
But as for prayer, or e're it faints,
Far better is the breath of saints
   Than galbanum and myrrh.

For Adoration from the down,
Of dam'sins to th' anana's crown,
   God sends to tempt the taste;
And while the luscious zest invites,
The sense, that in the scene delights,
   Commands desire be chaste.

For Adoration, all the paths
Of grace are open, all the baths
   Of purity refresh;
And all the rays of glory beam
To deck the man of God's esteem,
   Who triumphs o'er the flesh.

CHRISTOPHER SMART

Devotion to Avalokiteśvara*

O you, whose eyes are clear, whose eyes are friendly,
Whose eyes betray distinguished wisdom-knowledge;
Whose eyes are pitiful, whose eyes are pure,
O you, so lovable, with beautiful face, with beautiful eyes!

Your lustre is spotless and immaculate,
Your knowledge without darkness, your splendour like the sun,
Radiant like the blaze of a fire not disturbed by the wind,
Warming the world you shine splendidly.

Eminent in your pity, friendly in your words,
One great mass of fine virtues and friendly thoughts,
You appease the fire of the defilements which burn beings,
And you rain down the rain of the deathless Dharma.†

In quarrels, disputes and in strife,
In the battles of men, and in any great danger,
To recollect the name of Avalokiteśvara
Will appease the troops of evil foes.

His voice is like that of a cloud or drum;
Like a rain-cloud he thunders, sweet in voice like Brahma.‡
His voice is the most perfect that can be.
So one should recall Avalokiteśvara.

Think of him, think of him, without hesitation,
Of Avalokiteśvara, that pure being.
In death, disaster and calamity
He is the saviour, refuge and recourse.

As he who has reached perfection in all virtues,
Who looks on all beings with pity and friendliness,
Who is virtue itself, a great ocean of virtues,
As such Avalokiteśvara is worthy of adoration.

He who is now so compassionate to the world,
He will a Buddha be in future ages.
Humbly I bow to Avalokiteśvara
Who destroys all sorrow, fear and suffering.

SADDHARMAPUNDARIKA
Translated from the Sanskrit by Edward Conze

* Avalokiteśvara is the Buddha in his compassionate aspect
† *Dharma*: the teaching of Buddha
‡ *Brahma*: the Creator

Lord of the Ring

Our Lord, Lord of the Ring,
self-engendered, self-willing, self-enjoying;
even as He wills, so shall He desire that it shall be.
In the centre of the palm of His hand He has placed us,
He is moving us according to His pleasure.
We are moving and turning like children's marbles,
    tossed without direction.
To him we are an object of diversion: He laughs at us.

ANONYMOUS NAHUATL POEM
Translated from a Spanish version by Irene Nicholson

Gird on Thy Sword

Gird on thy sword and join in the fight!
Fight, O my brother, so long as life lasteth!
Strike off the enemy's head and there make an end of him quickly:
Then come, bow thyself in the King's Assembly.
A brave man leaveth not the battle;
He who flieth from it is no true warrior.
In the field of this body a great war is toward
Against Passion Anger Pride and Greed.
It is for the kingdom of Truth of Contentment and of
    Purity that this battle is raging:
And the sword that ringeth most loudly is the sword of His Name . . .

KABIR
Translator unknown, revised by Robert Bridges

125

PART SIX

Neither Existent nor Non-Existent

The Song of Creation

Then was not non-existent nor existent: there was no realm
of air, no sky beyond it.
What covered in, and where? and what gave shelter?
Was water there, unfathomed depth of water?

Death was not then, nor was their aught immortal: no sign
was there, the day's and night's divider.
That one thing, breathless, breathed by its own nature:
apart from it was nothing whatsoever.

Darkness there was: at first concealed in darkness, this All
was indiscriminated chaos.
All that existed then was void and formless: by the great
power of warmth was born that unit.

Thereafter rose desire in the beginning, Desire, the primal
seed and germ of spirit.
Sages who searched with their heart's thought discovered the
existent's kinship in the non-existent.

Transversely was their severing line extended: what was
above it then, and what below it?
There were begetters, there were mighty forces, free action
here and energy up yonder.

Who verily knows and who can here declare it, whence it
was born and whence comes this creation?
The gods are later than this world's production. Who
knows, then, whence it first came into being?

He, the first origin of this creation, whether he formed it all
or did not form it,
Whose eye controls this world in highest heaven, he verily
knows it, or perhaps he knows not.

From the *Rig-Veda*
Translated from the Sanskrit by F. Max Muller

From The Gospel According to St John

In the beginning was the Word, and the Word was with God, and the Word was God.

The same was in the beginning with God.

All things were made by him; and without him was not any thing made that was made.

In him was life; and the life was the light of men.

And the light shineth in darkness; and the darkness comprehended it not.

Chapter 1.1–5

From De Rerum Natura

Matter mingled and massed into indissoluble union
Does not exist. For we see how wastes each separate substance;
So flow piecemeal away, with the length'ning centuries, all things,
Till from our eye by degrees that old self passes, and is not.
Still Universal Nature abides unchanged as aforetime.
Whereof this is the cause. When the atoms part from a substance,
That suffers loss; but another is elsewhere gaining an increase:
So that, as one thing wanes, still a second bursts into blossom,
Soon, in its turn, to be left. Thus draws this Universe always
Gain out of loss; thus live we mortals one on another.
Burgeons one generation, and one fades. Let but a few years
Pass, and a race has arisen which was not: as in a racecourse,
One hands on to another the burning torch of Existence.

LUCRETIUS
Translated from the Latin by C. S. Calverley

Amergin

I am the wind which breathes upon the sea,
I am the wave of the ocean,
I am the murmur of the billows,
I am the ox of the seven combats,
I am the vulture upon the rocks,
I am a beam of the sun,
I am the fairest of plants,
I am a wild boar in valour.
I am a salmon in the water,
I am a lake in the plain,
I am a word of science,
I am the point of the lance in battle,
I am the God who creates in the head the fire.
Who is it who throws light into the meeting on the mountain?
Who announces the ages of the moon?
Who teaches the place where couches the sun?

ANONYMOUS

The Mystery

We uncovered a mystery. We slowly drew back the veil from its face
– there it lay, an unspecified form, overdue and precipitate, clearly
beyond comprehension, with something concealed in its core, and we
felt quite certain that this was a mystery and, as such, it had to be
probed and uncovered; with great care we drew back its veil, and now it
appeared before us, a genuine mystery – not paid for, nor ever
encountered – and gleamed like firewood which soon was to burn, and
we certainly wanted an insight and wanted to know; we drew back its
coverings, and uncovered the mystery: crosswise, it lay like a breeze that
was lost, and there was no knowing if it was weighty or merely
pretended to be so; or if it indeed was a mystery; if it was, though, we
had to uncover it; eager, all eyes, we uncovered the mystery: it now was

at last a genuine and more than genuine mystery, alarmingly small and becoming still smaller and smaller, and seemingly farther and farther away, and we feared we might lose the mystery, and no longer wished to uncover it.

We were left with strange veils in our hands. Like proof of our wish to uncover something or other.

IMANTS ZIEDONIS
From *Epiphanies*. Translated from the Latvian by Ruth Speirs

Pythagoras

Thou vainly, O Man, self-deceiver, exaltest
Thyself the king and only thinker of this world,
Where life aboundeth infinite to destroy thee.

Well-guided are thy forces and govern'd bravely,
But like a tyrant cruel or savage monster
Thou disregardest ignorantly all being
Save only thine own insubordinate ruling:

As if the flower held not a happy pact with Spring;
As if the brutes lack'd reason and sorrow's torment;
Or ev'n divine love from the small atoms grew not,
Their grave affection unto thy passion mingling.

An truly were it nobler and better wisdom
To fear the blind thing blindly, lest it espy thee;
And scrupulously do honour to dumb creatures,

No one offending impiously, nor forcing
To service of vile uses; ordering rather
Thy slave to beauty, compelling lovingkindness.

So should desire, the only priestess of Nature
Divinely inspir'd, like a good monarch rule thee,
And lead thee onward in the consummate motion
Of life eternal unto heav'nly perfection.

ROBERT BRIDGES

Reason and Imagination

The Negation is the Spectre, the Reasoning Power in Man:
This is a false Body, an Incrustation over my Immortal
Spirit, a Selfhood which must be put off and annihilated alway.
To cleanse the Face of my Spirit by self-examination,
To bathe in the waters of Life, to wash off the Not Human,
I come in Self-annihilation and the grandeur of Inspiration;
To cast off Rational Demonstration by Faith in the Saviour,
To cast off the rotten rags of Memory by Inspiration,
To cast off Bacon, Locke, and Newton from Albion's covering,
To take off his filthy garments and clothe him with Imagination;
To cast aside from Poetry all that is not Inspiration,
That it no longer shall dare to mock with the aspersion of Madness
Cast on the Inspirèd by the tame high finisher of paltry Blots
Indefinite or paltry Rhymes, or paltry Harmonies,
Who creeps into State Government like a caterpillar to destroy;
To cast off the idiot Questioner, who is always questioning,
But never capable of answering; who sits with a sly grin
Silent plotting when to question, like a thief in a cave;
Who publishes Doubt and calls it Knowledge; whose Science is Despair,
Whose pretence to knowledge is Envy, whose whole Science is
To destroy the wisdom of ages, to gratify ravenous Envy
That rages round him like a Wolf, day and night, without rest.
He smiles with condescension; he talks of Benevolence and Virtue,
And those who act with Benevolence and Virtue they murder time on
    time.

These are the destroyers of Jerusalem! these are the murderers
Of Jesus! who deny the Faith and mock at Eternal Life,
Who pretend to Poetry that they may destroy Imagination
By imitation of Nature's Images drawn from Remembrance.
These are the Sexual Garments, the Abomination of Desolation,
Hiding the Human Lineaments, as with an Ark and Curtains
Which Jesus rent, and now shall wholly purge away with Fire,
Till Generation is swallow'd up in Regeneration.

WILLIAM BLAKE
From *Milton*, f. 42, 1.34 – f. 43, 1.28

Mutability

Not even the trees. The tallest plane-trees
in Hyde Park seem cartographer's smudged marks
on an old map of London, hardly these
survivors of elaborate road-works.
How the concrete rises against the sky!
This air also has the finality
of abstraction: observe the water crease –
as if a horse's tail swished at a fly,

so little movement. All landscapes dissolve
no sooner than they seem memorable.
I shut my eyes on faces which I love
to make finer sensations possible:
mutability can appear absurd
when memory keeps an exact record.
And yet at times I too feel disabled,
forget a face or an important word.

Nothing really holds. Jets unlock their wheels
descending over London in a suspense
of diminishing motion. God, what it feels
like to be coming to a stop, or to sense
that one is never going to be the same!
The tall trees bewilder me with their calm.
To abstract from life a permanence
is art's process to which life has no claim.

ZULFIKAR GHOSE

From The Faerie Queene

Thus, all these fower (the which the ground-work bee
  Of all the world, and of all living wights)
  To thousand sorts of *Change* we subject see:
  Yet are they chang'd (by other wondrous slights)
  Into themselves, and lose their native mights;
  The Fire to Aire, and th'Aire to Water sheere,
  And Water into Earth: yet Water fights
  With Fire, and Aire with Earth approaching neere:
Yet all are in one body, and as one appeare.

So, in them all raignes *Mutabilitie*;
  How-ever these, that Gods themselves do call,
  Of them doe claime the rule and soveraity:
  As, *Vesta*, of the fire æthereall;
  Vulcan, of this, with us so usuall;
  Ops, of the earth; and *Iuno* of the Aire;
  Neptune, of Seas; and Nymphes, of Rivers all.
  For, all those Rivers to me subject are:
And all the rest, which they usurp, be all my share.

EDMUND SPENSER
From *The Faerie Queene*, 'Mutabilitie' (Canto vii, 25, 26)

Winter Night

My house is poor; those that I love have left me.
My body is sick; I cannot join the feast.
There is not a living soul before my eyes
As I lie alone locked in my cottage room.
My broken lamp burns with a feeble flame;
My tattered curtains are crooked and do not meet.
'Tsek, tsek' on the door-step and window-sill
Again I hear the new snow fall.
As I grow older, gradually I sleep less;
I wake at midnight and sit up straight in bed.
If I had not learned the 'art of sitting and forgetting',
How could I bear this utter loneliness?
Stiff and stark my body cleaves to the earth;
Unimpeded my soul yields to Change.
So has it been for four tedious years,
Through one thousand and three hundred nights!

PO CHÜ-I
Translated from the Chinese by Arthur Waley

The Comet

The comet, has it nerves or is it dead;
Has it a mind, or is it burning rock?

Some people believe in a world after death,
While others say we're only vegetables.

I advise you to avoid ugliness
And do what's good, for I've learnt the soul

Near death repents, repents its gouty skin
Which began so fresh, and may do again.

ABU-AL-'ALĀ' AL-MA'ARRI
Translated from the Arabic by George Wightman and Abdullah al-Udhari

From The Ancient Sage

Thou canst not prove the Nameless, O my son,
Nor canst thou prove the world thou movest in,
Thou canst not prove that thou art body alone,
Nor canst thou prove that thou art spirit alone,
Nor canst thou prove that thou art both in one:
Thou canst not prove thou art immortal, no
Nor yet that thou art mortal – nay my son,
Thou canst not prove that I, who speak with thee,
Am not thyself in converse with thyself,
For nothing worthy proving can be proven,
Nor yet disproven: wherefore thou be wise,
Cleave ever to the sunnier side of doubt,
And cling to Faith beyond the forms of Faith!

ALFRED, LORD TENNYSON

The Guru Speaks

To desire much bringeth a troubled mind;
So store within thy heart these precepts wise:
Many seeming Thats are not the That;
Many trees bear nought of Fruit;
All sciences are not the Wisdom true.
Much talking is of little profit
That which enricheth the heart is the Sacred Wealth.
Desirest thou Wealth, then store thou this;
The Doctrine which subdueth passions vile is the Noble Path;
Desirest thou a safe Path? then tread thou this.
Forsake the weeping sorrow-burdened world;
Make lonely caves thy home paternal,
And solitude thy paradise.
Let thought riding Thought be thy tireless steed,
And thy body thy temple filled with gods,
And ceaseless devotion thy best of drugs.
To thee, thou energetic one,

The Teaching that containeth all Wisdom I have given;
Thy Faith, the Teaching and myself are one.
And may this perfect Seed of Truth thus to my son entrusted,
Bring forth its foliage and its fruit,
Without corruption, without being scattered, without withering.

MILAREPA
Translated from the Tibetan by W. Y. Evans-Wentz

The Clod and the Pebble

'Love seeketh not itself to please,
Nor for itself hath any care,
But for another gives its ease,
And builds a Heaven in Hell's despair.'

So sung a little Clod of Clay,
Trodden with the cattle's feet,
But a Pebble of the brook
Warbled out these metres meet:

'Love seeketh only Self to please,
To bind another to its delight,
Joys in another's loss of ease,
And builds a Hell in Heaven's despite.'

WILLIAM BLAKE

Beyond Thought

'This is myself and this is another.'
Be free of this bond which encompasses you about,
And your own self is thereby released.

Do not err in this matter of self and other.
Everything is Buddha without exception.
Here is that immaculate and final stage,
Where thought is pure in its true nature.

The fair tree of thought that knows no duality,
Spreads through the triple world.
It bears the flower and fruit of compassion,
And its name is service of others.

The fair tree of the Void abounds with flowers,
Acts of compassion of many kinds,
And fruit for others appearing spontaneously,
For this joy has no actual thought of another.

So the fair tree of the Void also lacks compassion,
Without shoots or flowers or foliage,
And whoever imagines them there, falls down,
For branches there are none.

The two trees spring from one seed,
And for that reason there is but one fruit.
He who thinks of them thus indistinguishable,
Is released . . .

From *Saraha's Treasury of Songs*
Translated from the Tibetan by D. Snellgrove

The Divine Image

To Mercy, Pity, Peace, and Love
All pray in their distress;
And to these virtues of delight
Return their thankfulness.

For Mercy, Pity, Peace, and Love
Is God, our Father dear,
And Mercy, Pity, Peace, and Love
Is man, His child and care.

For Mercy has a human heart,
Pity a human face,
And Love, the human form divine,
And Peace, the human dress.

Then every man, of every clime,
That prays in his distress,
Prays to the human form divine,
Love, Mercy, Pity, Peace.

And all must love the human form,
In heathen, Turk, or Jew;
Where Mercy, Love, and Pity dwell
There God is dwelling too.

WILLIAM BLAKE

Aeneas Descends into Hell

On the level bosom of this vale more thickly the tall trees
Grow, an'aneath quivering poplars and whispering alders
Lethe's dreamy river throu' peaceful scenery windeth.
Whereby now flitted in vast swarms many people of all lands,
As when in early summer honey-bees on a flowery pasture

Pill the blossoms, hurrying to' an' fro – innumerous are they,
Revisiting the ravish'd lily cups, while all the meadow hums.
  Aeneas was turn'd to the sight, and marvelling inquired,
'Say, sir, what the river that there i' the vale-bottom I see?
And who they that thickly along its bank have assembled?'
  Then Lord Anchises, 'The spirits for whom a second life
And body are destined ar' arriving thirsty to Lethe,
And here drink th' unmindful draught from wells of oblivyon.
My heart greatly desired of this very thing to acquaint thee,
Yea, and show thee the men to-be-born, our glory her'after,
So to gladden thine heart where now thy voyaging endeth.'
'Must it then be-believ'd, my sire, that a soul which attaineth
Elysium will again submit to her old body-burden?
Is this well? what hap can awake such dire longing in them?'
'I will tell thee, O son, nor keep thy wonder awaiting,'
Answereth Anchises, and all expoundeth in order.
'Know first that the heavens, and th' Earth, and space fluid or void,
Night's palid orb, day's Sun, and all his starry coaevals,
Are by one spirit inly quickened, and, mingling in each part,
Mind informs the matter, nature's complexity ruling.
Thence the living creatures, man, brute, and ev'ry feather'd fowl,
And what breedeth in Ocean aneath her surface of argent:
Their seed knoweth a fiery vigour, 'tis of airy divine birth,
In so far as unimpeded by an alien evil,
Nor dull'd by the body's framework condemn'd to corruption.
Hence the desires and vain tremblings that assail them, unable
Darkly prison'd to arise to celestial exaltation;
Nor when death summoneth them anon earth-life to relinquish,
Can they in all discard their stain, nor wholly away with
Mortality's plaguespots. It must-be that, O, many wild graffs
Deeply at 'heart engrain'd have rooted strangely upon them:
Wherefore must suffering purge them, yea, Justice atone them
With penalties heavy as their guilt: some purify exposed
Hung to the viewless winds, or others long watery searchings
Low i' the deep wash clean, some bathe in fiery renewal:
Each cometh unto his own retribution – if after in ample
Elysium we attain, but a few, to the fair Happy Woodland,
Yet slow time still worketh on us to remove the defilement,

141

Till it hath eaten away the acquir'd dross, leaving again free
That first fiery vigour, the celestial virtue of our life.
All whom here thou seest, hav' accomplished purification:
Unto the stream of Lethe a god their company calleth,
That forgetful of old failure, pain and disappointment,
They may again into' earthly bodies with glad courage enter.'

VIRGIL
Aeneid, VI. 703–51. Translated from the Latin by Robert Bridges

The Trees of the Garden

Ye who have passed Death's haggard hills; and ye
   Whom trees that knew your sires shall cease to know
   And still stand silent: – is it all a show –
A wisp that laughs upon the wall? – decree
Of some inexorable supremacy
   Which ever, as man strains his blind surmise
   From depth to ominous depth, looks past his eyes,

Sphinx-faced with unabashèd augury?
Nay, rather question the Earth's self. Invoke
   The storm-felled forest-trees moss-grown to-day
   Whose roots are hillocks where the children play;
Or ask the silver sapling 'neath what yoke
Those stars, his spray-crown's clustering gems, shall wage
Their journey still when his boughs shrink with age.

DANTE GABRIEL ROSSETTI

The Swords of Glass

I turn in the morning to defy, as I pass
the shabby antique-shop window, the swords of glass:
a blue crossing a green, but on each hilt
a bine of crimson, a frozen braid of gilt
and of water-crystal. Their twin smooth tips are sharp
as briars; the blades though flute and twist and warp
like barley-sugar if it glittered, or the gold
shafts of a roundabout. Self-enclosed and cold,
they creep with childhood's nausea for the too
richly-confected plane that is not quite true.
As these are not: not toys, yet they would smash
to sharp confetti round the fighter; never a flash
in beauty or gallantry; they have never been
crossed, but in mocking rest, the blue and the green.

I know them, the nature of all glass, the old sky
shallowness of the goat's the parrot's and the Arab's eye:
the blind perspective sparkle. Glass is a liar:
the air of images, witch-water, the dead man's fire;
dark-diamonded room of earth, light without heat,
where dazzle of limbeck and hell of mirror meet.
Lies, they have stabbed at lies, and the gesture lied.
The blue sword entered drily a dust-bubble's side,
dust in damnation's effigy of a Christ; and there
an evil Nothing vainly crucified air.
Strong in the green sword, Satan leaned above a well,
stabbed his own image, flared like a nova, and fell.
Colours and acts met on the mirror's face:
hell's ingrown icicle, suicide of glass,
I turn in the morning to defy as I pass.

TERENCE TILLER

143

On Boundlessness

I seemed to learn
That what we see of forms and images
Which float along our minds, and what we feel
Of active or recognizable thought,
Prospectiveness, or intellect, or will,
Not only is not worthy to be deemed
Our being, to be prized as what we are,
But is the very littleness of life.
Such consciousness I deem but accidents,
Relapses from the one interior life
That lives in all things, sacred from the touch
Of that false secondary power by which
In weakness we create distinctions, then
Believe that all our puny boundaries are things
Which we perceive and not which we have made;
– In which all beings live with god, themselves
Are god, existing in the mighty whole,
As indistinguishable as the cloudless East
At noon is from the cloudless West, when all
The hemisphere is one cerulean blue.

WILLIAM WORDSWORTH
Ms fragment intended for *The Prelude*

On Reading the Dhyana Sutra

What I must learn is that all substances lack true
    substance;
To linger on the No-Residue is to make fresh Residue.
Forget the Word even while it is spoken, and there will be
    nothing you do not understand;
To tell your dream while still dreaming is to pile vanity
    on vanity.
How expect the flower-in-the-air also to produce fruit?
In mirage waters how suppose you will find real fish?
The suppression of movement is Dhyana; Dhyana itself is
    movement;
'No Dhyana, no movement' – that is the Truly So.

Po Chü-i
Texts originating in India. Translated from the Chinese by Arthur Waley

From De Rerum Natura

To possess, impregnably guarded,
Those calm heights of the sages, which have for
    an origin Wisdom;
Thence to survey our fellows, observe them this
    way and that way
Wander amidst Life's paths, poor stragglers seeking
    a highway:
Watch mind battle with mind, and escutcheon rival
    escutcheon;
Gaze on that untold strife, which is waged 'neath
    the sun and the starlight,
Up as they toil on the surface whereon rest Riches
    and Empire.
O race born unto trouble! O minds all lacking
    of eyesight!

145

'Neath what a vital darkness, amidst how terrible
    dangers,
Move ye thro' this thing, Life, this fragment! Fools,
    that ye hear not
Nature clamour aloud for the one thing only; that,
    all pain
Parted and past from the Body, the Mind too bask
    in a blissful
Dream, all fear of the future and all anxiety over!

LUCRETIUS
Translated from the Latin by C. S. Calverley

Shadows in the Water

In unexperienc'd Infancy
Many a sweet Mistake doth ly:
Mistake tho false, intending tru;
A *Seeming* somwhat more than View;
    That doth instruct the Mind
    In Things that ly behind,
And many Secrets to us show
Which afterwards we com to know.

Thus did I by the Water's brink
Another World beneath me think;
And while the lofty spacious Skies
Reversed there abus'd mine Eys,
    I fancy'd other Feet
    Came mine to touch and meet;
As by som Puddle I did play
Another World within it lay.

Beneath the Water Peeple drown'd
Yet with another Hev'n crown'd,
In spacious Regions seem'd to go
Freely moving to and fro:
   In bright and open Space
   I saw their very face;
Eys, Hands, and Feet they had like mine;
Another Sun did with them shine.

'Twas strange that Peeple there should walk,
And yet I could not hear them talk:
That throu a little watry Chink,
Which one dry Ox or Horse might drink,
   We other Worlds should see,
   Yet not admitted be;
And other Confines there behold
Of Light and Darkness, Heat and Cold.

I call'd them oft, but call'd in vain;
No Speeches we could entertain:
Yet did I there expect to find
Some other World, to pleas my Mind.
   I plainly saw by these
   A new *Antipodes*,
Whom, tho they were so plainly seen,
A Film kept off that stood between.

By walking Men's reversed Feet
I chanc'd another World to meet;
Tho it did not to View exceed
A Phantasm, 'tis a World indeed,
   Where Skies beneath us shine,
   And Earth by Art divine
Another face presents below,
Where Peeple's feet against Ours go.

Within the Regions of the Air,
Compass'd about with Hev'ns fair,
Great Tracts of Land there may be found
Enricht with Fields and fertil Ground;
   Where many num'rous Hosts,
   In those far distant Coasts,
For other great and glorious Ends,
Inhabit, my yet unknown Friends.

O ye that stand upon the Brink,
Whom I so near me, throu the Chink,
With Wonder see: What Faces there,
Whose Feet, whose Bodies, do ye wear?
   I my Companions see
   In you, another Me.
They seemed Others, but are We;
Our second Selvs those Shadows be.

Look how far off those lower Skies
Extend themselvs! scarce with mine Eys
I can them reach. O ye my Friends,
What *Secret* borders on those Ends?
   Are lofty Hevens hurl'd
   'Bout your inferior World?
Are ye the Representatives
Of other Peopl's distant Lives?

Of all the Play-mates which I knew
That here I do the Image view
In other Selvs; what can it mean?
But that below the purling Stream
   Som unknown Joys there be
   Laid up in Store for me;
To which I shall, when that thin Skin
Is broken, be admitted in.

THOMAS TRAHERNE

Certainty

If the white light of this lamp
is real, and real
the hand that writes,
are the eyes real
that look at what I write?

One word follows another.
What I saw vanishes.
I know that I am alive,
and living between two parentheses.

OCTAVIO PAZ
Translated from the Spanish by J. M. Cohen

The Nature of Life

There is always a man painting
his house-door,
a woman cutting the lawn,
an old man climbing to the garage roof,
a grass bear entering the yard,
a head cut off by the light,
a car pounding the nerves,
a machine-gun in the night
and another set up in the street.
You are always in my dream,
so am I and my children,
and when I wake up
the light is otherworldly,
shot through with a slight disquiet
at having glimpsed, at moments
a real wood.

BELKIS CUZA MALÉ
Translated from the Spanish by J. M. Cohen

Sudden Light

I have been here before,
But when or how I cannot tell:
I know the grass beyond the door,
The sweet keen smell,
The sighing sound, the lights around the shore.

You have been mine before, –
How long ago I may not know:
But just when at that swallow's soar
Your neck turned so,
Some veil did fall, – I knew it all of yore.

Has this been thus before?
And shall not thus time's eddying flight
Still with our lives our love restore
In death's despite,
And day and night yield one delight once more?

DANTE GABRIEL ROSSETTI

The Terraced Valley

In a deep thought of you and concentration
I came by hazard to a new region:
The unnecessary sun was not there,
The necessary earth lay without care –
For more than sunshine warmed the skin
Of the round world that was turned outside-in.

Calm sea beyond the terraced valley
Without horizon easily was spread,
As it were overhead,
Washing the mountain-spurs behind me:
The unnecessary sky was not there,
Therefore no heights, no deeps, no birds of the air.

Neat outside-inside, neat below-above,
Hermaphrodizing love.
Neat this-way-that-way and without mistake:
On the right hand could slide the left glove.
Neat over-under: the young snake
Through an unyielding shell his path could break.
Singing of kettles, like a singing brook,
Made out-of-doors a fireside nook.

But you, my love, where had you then your station?
Seeing that on this counter-earth together
We go not distant from each other;
I knew you near me in that strange region,
So searched for you, in hope to see you stand
On some near olive-terrace, in the heat,
The left-hand glove drawn on your right hand,
The empty snake's egg perfect at your feet –
But found you nowhere in the wide land,
And cried disconsolately, until you spoke
Immediate at my elbow, and your voice broke
This trick of time, changing the world about
To once more inside-in and outside-out.

ROBERT GRAVES

A Rose from the Garden

Day after day the wind carries away a rose from the garden: and the heart of the nightingale feels a new sorrow.

The law of Time is the same for all men: murmur not, and submit to its justice.

The falcon of death carries off in his talons, like a pigeon, all things that are born.

O friend! Set not thy heart on this world: for peace undisturbed is not possible here.

The tulip and hyacinth that blossom come from the earth; perhaps from the dust of a face that was lovely, with hyacinthlike scented hair.

Nothing has ever been built on the earth, that time has not changed its perfection.

Yester-day the garden and its flowers felt the gladness of the warbling of birds.

To-day the thorns alone remain, as if never a rose had bloomed in the garden.

This world is a bridge that leads to Eternity: the wise build not their homes on the bridge.

SADI
From Ode 405. Translated from the Persian; translator unknown

Here

My steps in this street
Echo
     In another street
Where
     I hear my steps
          Walking down this street
Where
Nothing is real but the mist.

OCTAVIO PAZ
Translated from the Spanish by J. M. Cohen

I've Known a Heaven

I've known a Heaven, like a Tent –
To wrap its shining Yards –
Pluck up its stakes, and disappear –
Without the sound of Boards
Or Rip of Nail – Or Carpenter –
But just the miles of Stare –
That signalize a Show's Retreat –
In North America –

No Trace – no Figment of the Thing
That dazzled, Yesterday,
No Ring – no Marvel –
Men, and Feats –
Dissolved as utterly –
As Bird's far Navigation
Discloses just a Hue –
A plash of Oars, a Gaiety –
Then swallowed up, of View.

EMILY DICKINSON

Visionary Moment

'Through the slush and the ruts of the roadway –
By the side of the dam of the stream;
Where the wet fishing-nets are drying,
The carriage jogs on, and I muse.

I muse and I look at the roadway,
At the damp and the dull grey weather,
At the shelving bank of the lake,
And the far-off smoke of the villages.

153

By the dam, with a cheerless face,
Is walking a tattered old Jew.
From the lake, with a splashing of foam,
The waters rush through the weir.

A little boy plays on a pipe,
He has made it out of a reed.
The startled wild-ducks have flown,
And call as they sweep from the lake.

Near the old tumbling-down mill
Some labourers sit on the grass.
An old worn horse in a cart
Is lazily dragging some sacks.

And I know it all, oh! so well,
Though I never have been here before,
The roof there, far away yonder,
And the boy, and the wood, and the weir,

And the mournful voice of the mill,
And the crumbling barn in the field –
I have been here and seen it before,
And forgotten it all long ago.

This very same horse plodded on,
It was dragging the very same sacks;
And under the mouldering mill
The labourers sat on the grass.

And the Jew, with his beard, walked by,
And the weir made just such a noise.
All this has happened before,
Only, I cannot tell when.'

ALEXEY TOLSTOY
Translated from the Russian by the Hon. Maurice Baring

Optical Illusion

The twinkling of an eye, and the boxes on the floor
Hang from the ceiling. Really they are not boxes,
But only certain black lines on white paper,
(The programme of an hour of magic and illusion)
And, but for the eye, not even black on white,
But a vast molecular configuration,
A tremor in the void, discord in silence.
Boehme agrees with Jasper Maskelyne
That all is magic in the mind of man.

The boxes, then, depending on my mind
Hang in the air or stand on solid ground;
Real or ideal, still spaces to explore:
Eden itself was only a *gestalt*.

My house, my rooms, the landscape of my world
Hang, like this honeycomb, upon a thought,
And breeding-cells still hatch within my brain
Winged impulses,
(And still the bees will have it that earth has flowers)
But the same dust is the garden and the desert.
Ambiguous nothingness seems all things and all places.

KATHLEEN RAINE

The Fountain

Don't say, don't say there is no water
to solace the dryness at our hearts.
I have seen

the fountain springing out of the rock wall
and you drinking there. And I too
before your eyes

found footholds and climbed
to drink the cool water.

The woman of that place, shading her eyes,
frowned as she watched – but not because
she grudged the water,

only because she was waiting
to see we drank our fill and were
refreshed.

Don't say, don't say there is no water.
That fountain is there among its scalloped
green and gray stones,

it is still there and always there
with its quiet song and strange power
to spring in us,
up and out through the rock.

DENISE LEVERTOV

Poem Written Shortly Before Death

The first day's sun
had asked
at the manifestation of new being –
Who are you?
No answer came.
Year after year went by,
The last sun of the day
The last question utters
On the western sea-shore
In the silent evening –
Who are you?
He gets no answer.

RABINDRANATH TAGORE

From The Kaṭha Upanishad

Death said: 'The good is one thing, the pleasant another; these two, having different objects, chain a man. It is well with him who clings to the good; he who chooses the pleasant, misses his end.

'The good and pleasant approach man: the wise goes round about them and distinguishes them. Yea, the wise prefers the good to the pleasant, but the fool chooses the pleasant through greed and avarice.

'Thou, O Nachiketas, after pondering all pleasures that are or seem delightful, hast dismissed them all. Thou hast not gone into the road that leadeth to wealth, in which many men perish.

'Wide apart and leading to different points are these two, ignorance, and what is known as wisdom. I believe Nachiketas to be one who desires knowledge, for even many pleasures did not tear thee away.

'Fools dwelling in darkness, wise in their own conceit, and puffed up with vain knowledge, go round and round, staggering to and fro, like blind men led by the blind.

'The hereafter never rises before the eyes of the careless child, deluded by the delusion of wealth. "This is the world," he thinks, "there is no other" – thus he falls again and again under my sway.

'He (the Self) of whom many are not even able to hear, whom many, even when they hear of him, do not comprehend; wonderful is a man, when found, who is able to teach him (the Self); wonderful is he who comprehends him, when taught by an able teacher.'

Translated from the Sanskrit by F. Max Muller

Rublev's Icon

Atheists guard the angels;
the Soviets treasure
that trinity of beings
Abraham addressed as 'Lord';
amid primitive violence
the man who painted them
tried to live a pure life.
Their tranquillity contains
excess; the people blow
kisses at the plate glass.
Guards, guarded and angels
make another trinity.

JOHN BATE

From The Cherubic Wanderer

God is omnipotent, but powerless still
to stop my heart desiring what it will.

*

Pray God, O man, for neither that nor this.
Whatever you pray for, that your idol is.

ANGELUS SILESIUS
Translated from the German by J. M. Cohen

Neither Manifest nor Hidden

O how may I ever express that secret word?
O how can I say, He is unlike this, He is like that?
If I should say, He is within me, the universe were shamed.
If I say, He is without me, it is false.
He maketh the inner & the outer worlds to be indivisibly one.
The conscious and the unconscious, both are his footstools.
He is neither manifest nor hidden:
He is neither revealed nor unrevealed:
There are no words to tell what He is.

KABIR
Translated by Rabindranath Tagore and revised by Robert Bridges

On Trust in his Heart

The Perfect Way is only difficult for those who pick and choose;
Do not like, do not dislike; all will then be clear.
Make a hairbreadth difference, and Heaven and Earth are set apart;
If you want the truth to stand clear before you, never be for or against.
The struggle between 'for' and 'against' is the mind's worst disease;
While the deep meaning is misunderstood, it is useless to meditate on
     Rest.
It is blank and featureless as space; it has no 'too little' or 'too much';
Only because we take and reject does it seem to us not to be so.
Do not chase after Entanglements as though they were real things,
Do not try to drive pain away by pretending that it is not real;
Pain, if you seek serenity in Oneness, will vanish of its own accord.
Stop all movement in order to get rest, and rest will itself be restless;
Linger over either extreme, and Oneness is for ever lost.
Those who cannot attain to Oneness in either case will fail:
To banish Reality is to sink deeper into the Real;
Allegiance to the Void implies denial of its voidness.
The more you talk about It, the more you think about It, the further
     from It you go;
Stop talking, stop thinking, and there is nothing you will not
     understand.
Return to the Root and you will find the Meaning;
Pursue the Light, and you will lose its source,
Look inward, and in a flash you will conquer the Apparent and the
     Void.
For the whirligigs of Apparent and Void all come from mistaken views;
There is no need to seek Truth; only stop having views.

TAKAKUSU XLVIII
Translated from the Chinese by Arthur Waley

PART SEVEN

Hail, Holy Light

To the Sun

His bright rays bear him up aloft, the god who knoweth all that lives,
Sūrya, that all may look on him.

The constellations pass away, like thieves, together with their beams,
Before the all-beholding Sun.

His herald rays are seen afar refulgent o'er the world of men,
Like flames of fire that burn and blaze.

Swift and all beautiful art thou, O Sūrya, maker of the light,
Illuming all the radiant realm.

Thou goest to the hosts of gods, thou comest hither to mankind,
Hither all light to behold.

With that same eye of thine wherewith thou lookest, brilliant Varuna,
Upon the busy race of men,

Traversing sky and wide mid-air, thou metest with thy beams our days,
Sun, seeing all things that have birth.

Seven bay steeds harnessed to thy car bear thee, O thou farseeing one,
God, Sūrya with the radiant hair.

Sūrya hath yoked the pure bright seven, the daughters of the car; with
    these,
His own dear team, he goeth forth.

Looking upon the loftier light above the darkness, we have come
To Sūrya, god among the gods, the light that is most excellent.

Rising this day, O rich in friends, ascending to the loftier heaven,
Sūrya, remove my heart's disease, take from me this my yellow hue.

To parrots and to starlings let us give away my yellowness
Or this my yellowness let us transfer to haritāla trees.

With all his conquering vigour, this Āditya hath gone up on high,
Giving my foe into mine hand: let me not be my foeman's prey.

From the *Rig-Veda*
Translated from the Sanskrit by Max Muller

Guardian Angels

And is there care in heaven? and is there love
   In heavenly spirits to these creatures base,
That may compassion of their evils move?
     There is: else much more wretched were the case
     Of men, than beasts. But, O! th' exceeding grace
Of highest God, that loves his creatures so,
   And all his works with mercy doth embrace,
That blessed angels he sends to and fro,
To serve to wicked man, to serve his wicked foe.

How oft do they their silver bowers leave,
   To come to succour us, that succour want?
How oft do they with golden pinions cleave
     The flitting skies, like flying pursuivant,
     Against foul fiends to aid us militant?
They for us fight, they watch and duly ward,
   And their bright squadrons round about us plant,
And all for love, and nothing for reward:
O! why should heavenly God to men have such regard?

EDMUND SPENSER
The Faerie Queene, II. viii. 1, 2

Hail, Holy Light

Hail, holy Light, ofspring of Heav'n first-born,
Or of th' Eternal Coeternal beam
May I express thee unblam'd? since God is light,
And never but in unapproached light
Dwelt from Eternitie, dwelt then in thee,
Bright effluence of bright essence increate.
Or hear'st thou rather pure Ethereal stream,
Whose Fountain who shall tell? before the Sun,
Before the Heavens thou wert, and at the voice
Of God, as with a Mantle didst invest
The rising world of waters dark and deep,
Won from the void and formless infinite.

JOHN MILTON
'Paradise Lost' iv. 1–12

From All Eternity

From all eternity the Beloved unveiled His beauty in the
solitude of the unseen;
He held up the mirror to His own face, He displayed His
loveliness to Himself.
He was both the spectator and the spectacle; no eye but His
had surveyed the Universe.
All was One, there was no duality, no pretence of 'mine'
or 'thine'.
The vast orb of Heaven, with its myriad incomings and
outgoings, was concealed in a single point.
The Creation lay cradled in the sleep of non-existence, like
a child ere it has breathed.
The eye of the Beloved, seeing what was not, regarded
nonentity as existent.
Although He beheld His attributes and qualities as a perfect
whole in His own essence,

Yet He desired that they should be displayed to Him in
  another mirror,
And that each one of His eternal attributes should become
  manifest accordingly in a diverse form.
Therefore He created the verdant fields of Time and Space
  and the life-giving garden of the world,
That every branch and leaf and fruit might show forth His
  various perfections.
The cypress gave a hint of His comely stature, the rose gave
  tidings of His beauteous countenance.
Wherever Beauty peeped out, Love appeared beside it;
  wherever Beauty shone in a rosy cheek, Love lit his
  torch from that flame.
Wherever Beauty dwelt in dark tresses, Love came and
  found a heart entangled in their coils.
Beauty and Love are as body and soul; Beauty is the
  mine and Love is the precious stone.
They have always been together from the very first; and
  never have they travelled but in each other's company.

JAMI
Translated from the Persian by R. A. Nicholson

Cock-Crowing

Father of lights! what Sunnie seed,
What glance of day hast thou confin'd
Into this bird? To all the breed
This busie Ray thou hast assign'd;
    Their magnetisme works all night,
    And dreams of Paradise and light.

Their eyes watch for the morning hue,
Their little grain expelling night
So shines and sings, as if it knew
The path unto the house of light.
  It seems their candle, howe'r done,
  Was tinn'd and lighted at the sunne.

If such a tincture, such a touch,
So firm a longing can impowre
Shall thy own image think it much
To watch for thy appearing hour?
  If a meer blast so fill the sail,
  Shall not the breath of God prevail?

O thou immortall light and heat!
Whose hand so shines through all this frame,
That by the beauty of the seat,
We plainly see, who made the same.
  Seeing thy seed abides in me,
  Dwell thou in it, and I in thee.

To sleep without thee, is to die;
Yea, 'tis a death partakes of hell:
For where thou dost not close the eye
It never opens, I can tell.
  In such a dark, Ægyptian border,
  The shades of death dwell and disorder.

If joyes, and hopes, and earnest throws,
And hearts, whose Pulse beats still for light
Are given to birds; who, but thee, knows
A love-sick souls exalted flight?
  Can souls be track'd by any eye
  But his, who gave them wings to flie?

Onely this Veyle which thou hast broke,
And must be broken yet in me,
This veyle, I say, is all the cloke
And cloud which shadows thee from me.
  This veyle thy full-ey'd love denies,
  And onely gleams and fractions spies.

O take it off! make no delay,
But brush me with thy light, that I
May shine unto a perfect day,
And warme me at thy glorious Eye!
  O take it off! or till it flee,
  Though with no Lilie, stay with me!

HENRY VAUGHAN

Songs of the Soul in Intimate Communication and Union with the Love of God

Oh flame of love so living,
How tenderly you force
To my soul's inmost core your fiery probe!
Since now you've no misgiving,
End it, pursue your course
And for our sweet encounter tear the robe!

Oh cautery most tender!
Oh gash that is my guerdon!
Oh gentle hand! Oh touch how softly thrilling!
Eternal life you render,
Raise of all debts the burden
And change my death to life, even while killing!

168

Oh lamps of fiery blaze
To whose refulgent fuel
The deepest caverns of my soul grow bright,
Late blind with gloom and haze,
But in this strange renewal
Giving to the belov'd both heat and light.

What peace, with love enwreathing,
You conjure to my breast
Which only you your dwelling place may call:
While with delicious breathings
In glory, grace, and rest,
So daintily in love you make me fall!

St John of the Cross
Translated from the Spanish by Roy Campbell

Aaron

Holinesse on the head,
Light and perfections on the breast,
Harmonious bells below, raising the dead
To leade them unto life and rest:
Thus are true Aarons drest.

Profanenesse in my head,
Defects and darkenesse in my breast,
A noise of passions ringing me for dead
Unto a place where is no rest:
Poore priest thus as I drest.

Onely another head
I have, another heart and breast,
Another musick, making live not dead,
Without whom I could have no rest:
In him I am well drest.

Christ is my onely head,
My alone onely heart and breast,
My onely musick, striking me ev'n dead;
That to the old man I may rest,
And be in him new drest.

So holy in my head,
Perfect and light in my deare breast,
My doctrine tun'd by Christ (who is not dead,
But lives in me while I do rest)
Come people; Aaron's drest.

GEORGE HERBERT

The Soul Selects

The soul selects her own Society –
Then – shuts the Door –
To her divine Majority –
Present no more –

Unmoved – she notes the Chariots – pausing –
At her low Gate –
Unmoved – an Emperor be kneeling
Upon her Mat –

I've known her - from an ample nation -
Choose One -
Then - close the Valves of her attention -
Like Stone -

EMILY DICKINSON

The Eucharist

The Holy Vessel, like a golden sun,
hangs in the air, a momentary splendour.
Here nothing can be heard but words in Greek.
A whole world's held in hands, like a mere apple.

The solemn zenith of the sacred office,
the July light on the circle under the dome,
Make us sigh from full hearts, released from time,
for that small meadow where time does not run.

Like an eternal noon, the Holy Vessel
expands. All share in it, and play and sing.
From each one's eyes the Eucharist spills over
shining with inextinguishable joy.

OSIP MANDELSTAM
Translated from the Russian by J. M. Cohen

Quickness

False life! a foil and no more, when
          Wilt thou be gone?
Thou foul deception of all men
That would not have the true come on.

Thou art a moon-like toil; a blind
          Self-posing state;
A dark contest of waves and wind;
A mere tempestuous debate.

Life is fixed, discerning light,
          A knowing joy;
No chance, or fit; but ever bright,
And calm and full, yet doth not cloy.

'Tis such a blissful thing, that still
          Doth vivify,
And shine and smile, and hath the skill
To please without Eternity.

Thou art a toilsome mole, or less,
          A moving mist;
But life is what none can express,
A quickness which my God hath kissed.

HENRY VAUGHAN

Release into Reality

True to the pledge He made me, our treaty of alliance,
God raised me into Reality.
All that attests to it now is below my consciousness
and outside my created personality.
Here it is my subconsciousness; down there it was the Way.

*

172

Make me one with the One, thou unique One,
in a true act of confession that God is one,
to which no path serves as Way! As I am potential Truth,
and actual Truth is my own potential, may our separateness cease to be!
So with the thunderbolt all is illumined
and bathed in the radiance of the storm.

*

I have two watchers (my ears) which observe that I love him; and two
others (my eyes) which observe that You see me.
No thought but of You crosses my secret heart; my tongue utters
nothing that is not the love of You.
Should I look to the East, You are the risen sun; to the West,
You are straight before me.
If I look upwards, You are what lies above, if downwards, You are
everywhere.
It is You that give everything its place, yet You have no place.
You are the whole of everything, yet are not perishable.
You are my heart, my spirit, my inspiration, the rhythm
of my breath and the kernel of my organic being.

From the *Divan* of HUSEIN IBN MANSUR AL-HALLAJ
Translated from a French version of the Arabic by J. M. Cohen

My Mind to Me a Kingdom Is

My mind to me a kingdom is
    Such perfect joy therin I find,
That it excels all other bliss
That world affords or grows by kind.
        Though much I want which most would have,
        Yet still my mind forbids to crave.

173

No princely pomp, no wealthy store,
No force to win the victory,
No wily wit to salve a sore,
No shape to feed a loving eye;
   To none of these I yield as thrall,
   For why? my mind doth serve for all.

I see how plenty suffers oft,
And hasty climbers soon do fall;
I see that those which are aloft
Mishap doth threaten most of all;
   They get with toil, they keep with fear;
   Such cares my mind could never bear.

Content I live, this is my stay,
I seek no more than may suffice,
I press to bear no haughty sway;
Look, what I lack my mind supplies.
   Lo, thus I triumph like a king,
   Content with that my mind doth bring.

Some have too much, yet still do crave,
I little have, and seek no more:
They are but poor, though much they have,
And I am rich with little store:
   They poor, I rich; they beg, I give;
   They lack, I leave; they pine, I live.

I laugh not at another's loss,
I grudge not at another's gain;
No worldly waves my mind can toss,
My state at one doth still remain.
   I fear no foe, I fawn no friend;
   I loathe not life, nor dread no end.

Some weigh their pleasure by their lust,
Their wisdom by their rage of will;
Their treasure is their only trust,
A cloaked craft their store of skill:
    But all the pleasure that I find
    Is to maintain a quiet mind.

My wealth is health and perfect ease,
My conscience clear my chief defence;
I neither seek by bribes to please,
Nor by desert to breed offence.
    Thus do I live, thus will I die;
    Would all did so, as well as I.

SIR EDWARD DYER

The Birds Find their King

Once more they ventured from the Dust to raise
Their Eyes – up to the Throne – into the Blaze,
And in the Centre of the Glory there
Beheld the Figure of – *Themselves* – as 'twere
Transfigured – looking to Themselves, beheld
The Figure on the Throne en-miracled,
Until their Eyes themselves and *That* between
Did hesitate which *Seer* was, which *Seen*;
They That, That They: Another, yet the Same;
Dividual, yet One: from whom there came
A Voice of awful Answer, scarce discern'd,
From *which* to Aspiration *whose* return'd
They scarcely knew; as when some Man apart
Answers aloud the Question in his Heart:
'The Sun of my Perfection is a Glass
Wherein from *Seeing* into *Being* pass

175

All who, reflecting as reflected see
Themselves in Me, and Me in them; not *Me*,
But all of Me that a contracted Eye
Is comprehensive of Infinity;
Nor yet *Themselves*: no Selves, but of The All
Fractions, from which they split and wither fall.
As Water lifted from the Deep, again
Falls back in individual Drops of Rain,
Then melts into the Universal Main.
All you have been, and seen, and done, and thought,
Not *You* but *I*, have seen and been and wrought:
I was the Sin that from Myself rebell'd;
I the Remorse that tow'rd Myself compell'd;
I was the Tajidar who led the Track;
I was the little Briar that pull'd you back:
Sin and Contrition – Retribution owed,
And cancell'd – Pilgrim, Pilgrimage, and Road,
Was but Myself toward Myself; and Your
Arrival but *Myself* at my own Door;
Who in your Fraction of Myself behold
Myself within the Mirror Myself hold
To see Myself in, and each part of Me
That sees himself, though drown'd, shall ever see.
Come you lost Atoms to your Centre draw,
And *be* the Eternal Mirror that you saw:
Rays that have wander'd into Darkness wide
Return, and back into your Sun subside.'

'AṬṬĀR
From *The Parliament of the Birds*. Translated by Edward FitzGerald

Glory to the Lord

We have drunk the Lord's sherbet, glory to the Lord,
We have crossed the sea of might, glory to the Lord.

We have journeyed safely across these mountains and woods,
These vineyards in our sight, glory to the Lord.

We were scorched, we are slaked, earthbound, now we are birds,
Together we take our flight, glory to the Lord.

Let us be reconciled, if strangers, let us meet,
If riders, amble together, glory to the Lord.

We've welled into a spring, we've rolled into a river,
We've overflowed to the sea, glory to the Lord.

When we stood at Taptuk's door, humbly to serve and to learn,
Yunus, we were green, we have ripened, glory to the Lord.

YUNUS EMRE
Translated from the Turkish by Nermin Menemencioğlu

Peace

Sweet Peace, where dost thou dwell? I humbly crave,
        Let me once know.
  I sought thee in a secret cave,
    And ask'd, if Peace were there.
A hollow winde did seem to answer, No:
        Go seek elsewhere.

I did; and going did a rainbow note:
        Surely, thought I,
  This is the lace of Peaces coat:
    I will search out the matter.
But while I lookt, the clouds immediately
        Did break and scatter.

Then went I to a garden, and did spy
           A gallant flower,
  The Crown Imperiall: Sure, said I,
    Peace at the root must dwell.
But when I digg'd, I saw a worm devoure
           What show'd so well.

At length I met a rev'rend good old man,
           Whom when for Peace
  I did demand, he thus began:
    There was a Prince of old
At Salem dwelt, who liv'd with good increase
           Of flock and fold.

He sweetly liv'd; yet sweetnesse did not save
           His life from foes.
  But after death out of his grave
    There sprang twelve stalks of wheat:
Which many wondring at, got some of those
           To plant and set.

It prosper'd strangely, and did soon disperse
           Through all the earth:
  For they that taste it do rehearse,
    That vertue lies therein,
A secret vertue bringing peace and mirth
           By flight of sinne.

Take of this grain, which in my garden grows,
           And grows for you;
  Make bread of it: and that repose
    And peace, which ev'ry where
With so much earnestnesse you do pursue,
           Is onely there.

GEORGE HERBERT

Peace

My soul, there is a country
 Far beyond the stars,
Where stands a wingèd sentry
 All skilful in the wars:
There above noise and danger
 Sweet Peace sits crowned with smiles,
And One born in a manger
 Commands the beauteous files.
He is thy gracious friend
 And – O my soul, awake! –
Did in pure love descend
 To die here for thy sake.
If thou canst get but thither,
 There grows the flower of Peace,
The Rose that cannot wither,
 Thy fortress, and thy ease.
Leave then thy foolish ranges
 For none can thee secure,
But one who never changes,
 Thy God, thy life, thy cure.

HENRY VAUGHAN

Departure

Up, O ye lovers, and away! 'Tis time to leave the world for aye.
Hark, loud and clear from heaven the drum of parting calls – let none
 delay!
The cameleer hath risen amain, made ready all the camel-train,
And quittance now desires to gain: why sleep ye, travellers, I pray?
Behind us and before there swells the din of parting and of bells;
To shoreless space each moment sails a disembodied spirit away.
From yonder starry lights, and through those curtain-awnings darkly
 blue,

179

Mysterious figures float in view, all strange and secret things display.

From this orb, wheeling round its pole, a wondrous slumber o'er thee stole:

O weary life that weighest naught, O sleep that on my soul dost weigh!

O heart, toward thy heart's love wend, and O friend, fly toward the Friend,

Be wakeful, watchman, to the end: drowse seemingly no watchman may.

From the *Mathnawī* of RŪMĪ
Translated from the Persian by R. A. Nicholson

The Wine of Ecstasy

Drink wine that it may set you free from yourself . . .
Drink wine, for its cup is the face of the Friend
The cup is His eye drunken and flown with wine.
Seek wine without cup or goblet
Pure wine is that which gives you purification
from the stain of existence at the time of intoxication . . .
The whole universe is as His winehouse,
the heart of every atom as His winecup.
Reason is drunken, angels drunken, soul drunken,
air drunken, earth drunken, heaven drunken.

From *The Mystic Rose-Garden* of MAHMUD SHABISTARI
Translated from the Persian by E. H. Whitfield

To Tirzah*

Whate'er is Born of Mortal Birth,
Must be consumed with the Earth
To rise from Generation free;
Then what have I to do with thee?

The Sexes sprung from Shame & Pride
Blow'd in the morn: in evening died
But Mercy changed Death into Sleep;
The Sexes rose to work & weep.

Thou Mother of my Mortal part
With cruelty didst mould my Heart,
And with false self-deceiving tears,
Didst bind my Nostrils Eyes & Ears.

Didst close my Tongue in senseless clay
And me to Mortal Life betray:
The Death of Jesus set me free,
Then what have I to do with thee?

WILLIAM BLAKE

*Tirzah is nature, also the human mother

Songs of the Soul in Rapture at Having Arrived at the Height of Perfection, Which is Union with God by the Road of Spiritual Negation

Upon a gloomy night,
With all my cares to loving ardours flushed,
(O venture of delight!)
With nobody in sight
I went abroad when all my house was hushed.

181

In safety, in disguise,
In darkness up the secret stair I crept,
(O happy enterprise!)
Concealed from other eyes
When all my house at length in silence slept.

Upon that lucky night
In secrecy, inscrutable to sight,
I went without discerning
And with no other light
Except for that which in my heart was burning.

It lit and led me through
More certain than the light of noonday clear
To where One waited near
Whose presence well I knew,
There where no other presence might appear.

Oh night that was my guide!
Oh darkness dearer than the morning's pride,
Oh night that joined the lover
To the beloved bride
Transfiguring them each into the other.

Within my flowering breast
Which only for himself entire I save
He sank into his rest
And all my gifts I gave
Lulled by the airs with which the cedars wave.

Over the ramparts fanned
While the fresh wind was fluttering his tresses,
With his serenest hand
My neck he wounded, and
Suspended every sense with its caresses.

Lost to myself I stayed
My face upon my lover having laid
From all endeavour ceasing:
And all my cares releasing
Threw them amongst the lilies there to fade.

ST JOHN OF THE CROSS
Translated from the Spanish by Roy Campbell

The World

I saw Eternity the other night
Like a great *Ring* of pure and endless light,
    All calm, as it was bright,
And round beneath it, Time in hours, days, years
    Driv'n by the spheres
Like a vast shadow mov'd, In which the world
    And all her train were hurl'd;
The doting Lover in his queintest strain
    Did there Complain,
Neer him, his Lute, his fancy, and his flights,
    Wits sour delights,
With gloves, and knots the silly snares of pleasure;
    Yet his dear Treasure
All scatter'd lay, while he his eyes did pour
    Upon a flowr.

The darksome States-man, hung with weights and woe,
Like a thick midnight-fog mov'd there so slow
    He did nor stay, nor go;
Condemning thoughts (like sad Ecclipses) scowl
    Upon his soul,
And Clouds of crying witnesses without
    Pursued him with one shout.
Yet digg'd the Mole, and lest his ways be found
    Workt under ground,

Where he did Clutch his prey, but one did see
  That policie;
Churches and altars fed him, Perjuries
  Were gnats and flies,
It rain'd about him blood and tears, but he
  Drank them as free.

The fearfull miser on a heap of rust
Sate pining all his life there, did scarce trust
  His own hands with the dust,
Yet would not place one peece above, but lives
  In feare of theeves.
Thousands there were as frantick as himself
  And hugg'd each one his pelf,
The down-right Epicure plac'd heav'n in sense
  And scornd pretence

While others slipt into a wide Excesse
  Said little lesse;
The weaker sort slight, triviall wares inslave
  Who think them brave,
And poor, despised truth sate Counting by
  Their victory.

Yet some, who all this while did weep and sing,
And sing, and weep, soar'd up into the *Ring*,
  But most would use no wing.
O fools (said I,) thus to prefer dark night
  Before true light,
To live in grots, and caves, and hate the day
  Because it shews the way,
The way which from this dead and dark abode
  Leads up to God,
A way where you might tread the Sun, and be
  More bright than he.
But as I did their madness so discusse
  One whisper'd thus,
This Ring the Bride-groome did for none provide
  But for his bride.

HENRY VAUGHAN

Conversation at the Door

He asked: Who standeth at my door? I said: Thy
  indigent slave.
He asked: What dost thou here? I said: I am come
  to greet Thee, O my Lord.
He asked: How long wilt thou persist? I said: Until
  Thou call me in.
He asked: How long wilt thou desire it? I said: Till
  the last day of time, O Lord.
I laid claim to his Love; I took solemn oath that for
  love of Him I had renounc't wealth and power.
He asked: Doth not a judge demand a witness to prove
  a claim?
  I said: Tears are my witnesses, and my pale face the
    evidence.
He asked: Is thy witness trustworthy, when thine eyes
  are wayward?
  I said: I swear by thy great Justice, they are pure
    and free from sin.
He asked: What desirest thou of me? I said: Thy
  Constancy and Friendship. . . .
He asked: Who was thy Comrade? I said: The thought
  of Thee, O King.
He asked: Who call'd thee hither? I said: The rumour
  of thy Feast. . . .

O ask ye no more of me. Were I to tell you more
  words of his,
Ye would burst your bonds; no roof nor door could
  restrain you.

RŪMĪ
Translated from the Persian by Hasan Shahid Suhrawardy and revised by
Robert Bridges

In Praise of the Wine of Enlightenment

Come, for our hopes are no more than a jerry-built house:
Bring wine, for life's foundations are rooted in wind.

But that man's zeal shall draw me, which under this blue ceiling
Burns bright for nothing that ties us down to the world.

How can I tell you what good news the angel of the Unseen
Brought me last night, flat-out on the wine-shop's floor? –

'O royal keen-eyed falcon, whose perch is on the Tree of Life,
Why is this corner of affliction's town your nest?

'They are whistling you home from the battlements of the Empyrean:
What could you be doing here in this place of snares?'

Take my advice, and follow out what I say –
This is a dictum the Master has handed down:

Don't let the world's ill harm you – (note this, a subtlety
From one who had travelled far upon love's way) –

But accept whatever is dealt you – unknit your brows:
We shall find no other way out; free choice is not ours.

Don't look to hold this tottering world to her bond:
She is the withered hag of a thousand bridegrooms.

There is no faith in the smile of the rose:
Lament, empassioned nightingale: there is room for complaint.

Why should poetasters be jealous of Hafiz?
To please by subtleties of speech is the gift of God.

HAFIZ
Translated from the Persian by Peter Avery and John Heath-Stubbs

I Came Out Alone

I came out alone on my way to my tryst.
But who is this that follows me in the silent dark?
I move aside to avoid his presence but I escape him not.
He makes the dust rise from the earth with his swagger;
    he adds his loud voice to every word that I utter.
He is my own little self, my lord, he knows no shame;
    but I am ashamed to come to thy door in his company.

RABINDRANATH TAGORE

The True Vision

I am running towards the fountain of true life;
therefore, I spurn the life of lies and trifles.
To look at the face of my King – that is my only
wish. None but Him do I fear and venerate. If
only I could see Him in a dream! Oh, I would sleep
forever and never wake up. If I could see His face
inside my heart, my eyes would no more wish to look
outside.

JUDAH HALEVI
Translated from the Hebrew by T. Carmi

The Spirit of the Quest

O friend, hope in Him while thou livest, know Him while thou
    livest,
For in life is thy release.

If thy bonds be not broken while thou livest,
What hope of deliverance in death?

187

It is but an empty dream that the soul must pass into union with
    Him,
Because it hath passed from the body.

If He is found now, He is found then:
If not, we go but to dwell in the city of Death.

If thou hast union now, thou shalt have it hereafter.

Bathe in the Truth: know the true Master:
Have faith in the true Name.

Kabir saith: It is the spirit of the quest that helpeth.
I am the slave of the spirit of the quest.

KABIR
Translated by Rabindranath Tagore and revised by Robert Bridges

Dear City of God

I am at one with everything, O Universe,
    which is well-fitting in thee.
Nothing to me is early or late which is timely with thee.
    All is fruit to me that thy seasons bring.
    O Nature, from thee are all things,
      in thee are all things,
      to thee all things return.
    The poet saith, Dear city of Cecrops;
    shall not I say, Dear City of God.

MARCUS AURELIUS
Translated from the Latin by Robert Bridges

News

News from a forein Country came,
As if my Treasures and my Joys lay there;
So much it did my Heart enflame,
'Twas wont to call my Soul into mine Ear;
Which thither went to meet
Th' approaching Sweet,
And on the Threshold stood
To entertain the secret Good;
It hover'd there
As if 'twould leav mine Ear,
And was so eager to embrace
Th' expected Tidings, as they came,
That it could change its dwelling-place
To meet the voice of Fame.

As if new Tidings were the Things
Which did comprise my wished unknown Treasure,
Or els did bear them on their wings,
With so much Joy they came, with so much Pleasure,
My Soul stood at the Gate
To recreäte
It self with Bliss, and woo
Its speedier Approach; a fuller view
If fain would take,
Yet Journeys back would make
Unto my Heart, as if 'twould fain
Go out to meet, yet stay within,
Fitting a place to entertain
And bring the Tidings in.

What Sacred Instinct did inspire
My Soul in Childhood with an hope so strong?
What secret Force mov'd my Desire
T' expect my Joys beyond the Seas, so young?
Felicity I knew
Was out of view;

And being left alone,
I thought all Happiness was gon
    From Earth: for this
    I long'd-for absent Bliss,
Deeming that sure beyond the Seas,
Or els in somthing near at hand
Which I knew not, since nought did pleas
    I knew, my Bliss did stand.

But little did the Infant dream
That all the Treasures of the World were by,
    And that himself was so the Cream
And Crown of all which round about did ly.
        Yet thus it was! The Gem,
        The Diadem,
    The Ring enclosing all
That stood upon this Earthen Ball;
        The hev'nly Ey,
        Much wider than the Sky,
Wherin they All included were;
The Lov, the Soul, that was the King
Made to possess them, did appear
    A very little Thing.

THOMAS TRAHERNE

The Triumph of the Soul

Joy! joy! I triumph! now no more I know
Myself as simply me, I burn with love
Unto myself, and bury me in love.
The Centre is within me and its wonder
Lies as a circle everywhere about me.
Joy! joy! no mortal thought can fathom me.
I am the merchant and the pearl at once.
Lo, Time and Space lie crouching at my feet.
Joy! joy! when I would revel in a rapture,
I plunge into myself and all things know.

'ATṬĀR
From the *Jawhar Al-Dhāt*
Translated from the Persian by Margaret Smith

The Spirit of the Saints

There is a Water that flows down from Heaven
To cleanse the world of sin by grace Divine.
At last, its whole stock spent, its virtue gone,
Dark with pollution not its own, it speeds
Back to the Fountain of all purities;
Whence, freshly bathed, earthward it sweeps again,
Trailing a robe of glory bright and pure.

This Water is the Spirit of the Saints,
Which ever sheds, until itself is beggared,
God's balm on the sick soul; and then returns
To Him who made the purest light of Heaven.

From the *Mathnawī* of RŪMĪ
Translated from the Persian by R. A. Nicholson

Resurrection

Often we stand up,
stand up resurrected,
in the middle of the day,
with our living hair
and our breathing skin.

Nothing unusual around us,
no mirage of palms
with grazing lions
and gentle wolves.

The alarm-clocks do not stop ticking,
their illuminated hands do not go dark.

And yet insubstantial,
and yet safe from all wounds,
drawn up in secret order,
we are carried forward to a house of light.

MARIE-LUISE KASCHNITZ
Translated from the German by J. M. Cohen

The True Saint

He is the true Saint, who can reveal the form of the
    formless to the vision of these eyes:
Who teacheth the simple way of attaining Him,
    that is other than rites and ceremonies:
Who requireth thee not to close the doors,
    to hold the breath, and renounce the world:
Who maketh thee perceive the supreme Spirit
    wherever the mind resteth:
Who teacheth thee to be still amidst all thine activities:
Who, ever immersed in bliss, having no fear,
    keepeth the spirit of union thro'out all enjoyments . . .

KABIR
Translated by Rabindranath Tagore and revised by Robert Bridges

Written by a Zen Monk in Prison

Through all Heaven and Earth, no ground to plant my single
    staff;
Yet is there a place to hide this body where no trace may be
    found.
At midnight will the wooden man mount his steed of stone
To crash down ten thousand walls of encircling iron.

In the nothingness of man I delight, and of all being,
A thousand worlds complete in my little cage.
I forget sin, demolish my heart, and in enlightenment rejoice;
Who tells me that the fallen suffer in Hell's bonds?

Awful is the three-foot sword of the Great Yüan,
Sparkling with cold frost over ten thousand miles.
Though the skull be dry, these eyes shall see again.
Flawless is my white gem, priceless as a kingdom.

Like lightning it flashes through the shadows, severing the spring
    wind;
The God of Nothingness bleeds crimson, streaming.
I tremble at the soaring heights of Mount Sumera;
I will dive, I will leap into the stem of the lotus.

Sesson Yūbai
Translated from the Chinese by Burton Watson

From The Four Zoas

'Rise, sluggish Soul! Why sitt'st thou here? why does thou sit and
    weep?
Yon Sun shall wax old and decay, but thou shalt ever flourish.
The fruit shall ripen and fall down, and the flowers consume away,
But thou shalt still survive. Arise! O dry thy dewy tears!'

'Ha! shall I still survive? Whence came that sweet and comforting
        voice,
And whence that voice of sorrow? O Sun! thou art nothing now to me:
Go on thy course rejoicing, and let us both rejoice together!
I walk among His flocks and hear the bleating of His lambs.
O! that I could behold His face and follow His pure feet!
I walk by the footsteps of His flocks. Come hither, tender flocks!
Can you converse with a pure Soul that seeketh for her Maker?
You answer not: then am I set your mistress in this garden.
I'll watch you and attend your footsteps. You are not like the birds
That sing and fly in the bright air; but you do lick my feet,
And let me touch your woolly backs: follow me as I sing;
For in my bosom a new Song arises to my Lord:
"Rise up, O Sun! most glorious minister and light of day!
Flow on, ye gentle airs, and bear the voice of my rejoicing!
Wave freshly, clear waters, flowing around the tender grass;
And thou, sweet-smelling ground, put forth thy life in fruit and
        flowers!
Follow me, O my flocks, and hear me sing my rapturous song!
I will cause my voice to be heard on the clouds that glitter in the sun.
I will call, and who shall answer me? I shall sing; who shall reply?
For, from my pleasant hills, behold the living, living springs,
Running among my green pastures, delighting among my trees!
I am not here alone: my flocks, you are my brethren;
And you birds, that sing and adorn the sky, you are my sisters.
I sing, and you reply to my song; I rejoice, and you are glad.
Follow me, O my flocks! we will now descend into the valley.
O, how delicious are the grapes, flourishing in the sun!
How clear the spring of the rock, running among the golden sand!
How cool the breezes of the valley! And the arms of the branching trees
Cover us from the sun: come and let us sit in the shade." '

WILLIAM BLAKE
Night, IX, lines 416–448

Revelation

Two perhaps three
times
I was sure
I would touch the essence
and would know

the web of my formula
made of allusions as in the Phaedo
had also the rigour
of Heisenberg's equation

I was sitting immobile
with watery eyes
I felt my backbone
fill with quiet certitude

earth stood still
heaven stood still
my immobility
was nearly perfect

    the postman rang
    I had to pour out the dirty water
    prepare tea

    Siva lifted his finger
    the furniture of heaven and earth
    started to spin again

    I returned to my room
    where is that perfect peace
    the idea of a glass
    was being spilled all over the table

    I sat down immobile
    with watery eyes
    filled with emptiness
    i.e. with desire

If it happens to me once more
I shall be moved neither by the postman's bell
nor by the shouting of angels

I shall sit
immobile
my eyes fixed
upon the heart of things

a dead star

a black drop of infinity

Zbigniew Herbert
Translated from the Polish by Czeslaw Milosz and Peter Dale Scott

Intimations of Immortality from Recollections of Early Childhood

The Child is Father of the Man;
And I could wish my days to be
Bound each to each by natural piety.

There was a time when meadow, grove, and stream,
The earth, and every common sight,
        To me did seem
    Apparelled in celestial light,
The glory and the freshness of a dream.
It is not now as it hath been of yore; –
        Turn wheresoe'er I may,
            By night or day,
The things which I have seen I now can see no more.

The Rainbow comes and goes,
And lovely is the Rose;
The Moon doth with delight
Look round her when the heavens are bare;
Waters on a starry night
Are beautiful and fair;
The Sunshine is a glorious birth;
But yet I know, where'er I go,
That there hath past away a glory from the earth.

Now, while the birds thus sing a joyous song,
And while the young lambs bound
As to the tabor's sound
To me alone there came a thought of grief:
A timely utterance gave that thought relief,
And I again am strong:
The cataracts blow their trumpets from the steep;
No more shall grief of mine the season wrong;
I hear the Echoes through the mountains throng,
The Winds come to me from the fields of sleep,
And all the earth is gay;
Land and sea
Give themselves up to jollity,
And with the heart of May
Doth every Beast keep holiday; –
Thou Child of Joy,
Shout round me, let me hear thy shouts, thou happy
Shepherd-boy!

Ye blessed Creatures, I have heard the call
Ye to each other make; I see
The heavens laugh with you in your jubilee;
My heart is at your festival,
My head hath its coronal,
The fulness of your bliss, I feel – I feel it all.
Oh evil day! if I were sullen
While Earth herself is adorning,

This sweet May-morning,
And the Children are culling
On every side,
In a thousand valleys far and wide,
Fresh flowers; while the sun shines warm,
And the Babe leaps up on his Mother's arm: –
I hear, I hear, with joy I hear!
– But there's a Tree, of many, one,
A single Field which I have looked upon,
Both of them speak of something that is gone:
The Pansy at my feet
Doth the same tale repeat:
Wither is fled the visionary gleam?
Where is it now, the glory and the dream?

Our birth is but a sleep and a forgetting:
The Soul that rises with us, our life's Star,
Hath had elsewhere its setting,
And cometh from afar:
Not in entire forgetfulness,
And not in utter nakedness,
But trailing clouds of glory do we come
From God, who is our home:
Heaven lies about us in our infancy!
Shades of the prison-house begin to close
Upon the growing Boy,
But He
Beholds the light, and whence it flows,
He sees it in his joy;
The Youth, who daily farther from the east
Must travel, still is Nature's Priest,
And by the vision splendid
Is on his way attended;
At length the Man perceives it die away,
And fade into the light of common day.

Earth fills her lap with pleasures of her own;
Yearnings she hath in her own natural kind,
And, even with something of a Mother's mind,
  And no unworthy aim,
  The homely Nurse doth all she can
To make her Foster-child, her Inmate Man,
  Forget the glories he hath known,
And that imperial palace whence he came.

Behold the Child among his new-born blisses,
A six years' Darling of a pigmy size!
See, where 'mid work of his own hand he lies,
Fretted by sallies of his mother's kisses,
With light upon him from his father's eyes!
See, at his feet, some little plan or chart,
Some fragment from his dream of human life,
Shaped by himself with newly-learnèd art;
    A wedding or a festival,
    A mourning or a funeral;
      And this hath now his heart,
    And unto this he frames his song:
      Then will he fit his tongue
To dialogues of business, love, or strife;
    But it will not be long
    Ere this be thrown aside,
    And with new joy and pride
The little Actor cons another part;
Filling from time to time his 'humorous stage'
With all the Persons, down to palsied Age,
That Life brings with her in her equipage;
    As if his whole vocation
    Were endless imitation.

Thou, whose exterior semblance doth belie
    Thy Soul's immensity;
Thou best Philosopher, who yet dost keep
Thy heritage, thou Eye among the blind,
That, deaf and silent, read'st the eternal deep,

Haunted for ever by the eternal mind, –
   Mighty Prophet! Seer blest!
      On whom those truths do rest,
Which we are toiling all our lives to find,
In darkness lost, the darkness of the grave;
Thou, over whom thy Immortality
Broods like the Day, a Master o'er a Slave,
A Presence which is not to be put by;
Thou little Child, yet glorious in the might
Of heaven-born freedom on thy being's height,
Why with such earnest pains dost thou provoke
The years to bring the inevitable yoke,
Thus blindly with thy blessedness at strife?
Full soon thy Soul shall have her earthly freight,
And custom lie upon thee with a weight,
Heavy as frost, and deep almost as life!

     O joy! that in our embers
     Is something that doth live,
     That nature yet remembers
      What was so fugitive!
The thought of our past years in me doth breed
Perpetual benediction: not indeed
For that which is most worthy to be blest;
Delight and liberty, the simple creed
Of Childhood, whether busy or at rest,
With new-fledged hope still fluttering in his breast: –
     Not for these I raise
     The song of thanks and praise;
    But for those obstinate questionings
    Of sense and outward things,
    Fallings from us, vanishings;
    Blank misgivings of a Creature
Moving about in worlds not realized,
High instincts before which our mortal Nature
Did tremble like a guilty Thing surprised:
     But for those first affections,
     Those shadowy recollections,

Which, be they what they may,
Are yet the fountain light of all our day,
Are yet a master light of all our seeing;
    Uphold us, cherish, and have power to make
Our noisy years seem moments in the being
Of the eternal Silence: truths that wake,
        To perish never;
Which neither listlessness, nor mad endeavour,
        Nor Man nor Boy,
Nor all that is at enmity with joy,
Can utterly abolish or destroy!
        Hence in a season of calm weather
        Though inland far we be,
Our Souls have sight of that immortal sea
        Which brought us hither,
    Can in a moment travel thither,
And see the Children sport upon the shore,
And hear the mighty waters rolling evermore.

Then sing, ye Birds, sing, sing a joyous song!
        And let the young Lambs bound
        As to the tabor's sound!
We in thought will join your throng,
        Ye that pipe and ye that play,
        Ye that through your hearts today
        Feel the gladness of the May!
What though the radiance which was once so bright
Be now for ever taken from my sight,
        Though nothing can bring back the hour
Of splendour in the grass, of glory in the flower;
        We will grieve not, rather find
        Strength in what remains behind;
        In the primal sympathy
        Which having been must ever be;
        In the soothing thoughts that spring
        Out of human suffering;
        In the faith that looks through death,
In years that bring the philosophic mind.

And O, ye Fountains, Meadows, Hills, and Groves,
Forebode not any severing of our loves!
Yet in my heart of hearts I feel your might;
I only have relinquished one delight
To live beneath your more habitual sway.
I love the Brooks which down their channels fret,
Even more than when I tripped lightly as they;
The innocent brightness of a new-born Day
             Is lovely yet;
The Clouds that gather round the setting sun
Do take a sober colouring from an eye
That hath kept watch o'er man's mortality;
Another race hath been, and other palms are won.
Thanks to the human heart by which we live,
Thanks to its tenderness, its joys, and fears,
To me the meanest flower that blows can give
Thoughts that do often lie too deep for tears.

WILLIAM WORDSWORTH

From The Cherubic Wanderer

Be ye lamps unto yourselves,
Be your own radiance.

       *

Hold to the truth within yourselves
as to the only lamp.

       *

I am a single drop. How can it be
That the whole ocean, God, flows into me?

ANGELUS SILESIUS
Translated from the German by J. M. Cohen

Ascent into Paradise

'Thou'rt not on earth, as thou supposest thee:
    But lightning from its own place rushing out
    Ne'er sped as thou, who to thy home doest flee.'
If I was stript of my first teasing doubt
    By the brief smiling little words, yet freed
    I was not, but enmeshed in a new thought.
And I replied: 'I am released indeed
    From much amazement; yet am still amazed
    That those light bodies I transcend in speed.'
She, sighing in pity, gave me as she gazed
    The look that by a mother is bestowed
    Upon her child in its delirium crazed,
And said: 'All things, whatever their abode,
    Have order among themselves; this Form it is
    That makes the universe like unto God.
Here the high beings see the imprint of His
    Eternal power, which is the goal divine
    Whereto the rule aforesaid testifies.
In the order I speak of, all natures incline
    Either more near or less near to their source
    According as their diverse lots assign.
To diverse harbours thus they move perforce
    O'er the great ocean of being, and each one
    With instinct given it to maintain its course.
This bears the fiery element to the moon;
    This makes the heart of mortal things to move;
    This knits the earth together into one.
Not only creatures that are empty of
    Intelligence this bow shoots towards the goal,
    But those that have both intellect and love.
The Providence, that rules this wondrous whole,
    With its own light makes the heaven still to stay
    Wherein whirls that which doth the swiftest roll.'

DANTE ALIGHIERI
Paradiso, i. 91–123. Translated from the Italian by Laurence Binyon

From The Cherubic Wanderer

Let go and you snare God. But letting God go too
Is more than any but the rarest man can do.

Angelus Silesius
Translated from the German by J. M. Cohen

PART EIGHT

Now is Well

To Viracocha

Lord, creator
of the upper world
and the lower,
and of the widespreading ocean,
conqueror of all things
that gazes incessantly,
that seethes in its depths,
that this man may be,
that this woman may be
with commanding voice you say
to this true woman:
'I shaped you.'
Who are you, Lord,
where are you?
What is your purpose?
Speak to me!

QUECHUA HYMN
Translated from a Spanish version by J. M. Cohen

Hymn to Vāyu

O the Wind's chariot, O its power and glory! Crashing it
goes and hath a voice of thunder.
It makes the regions red and touches heaven, and as it moves
the dust of earth is scattered.

Along the traces of the Wind they hurry, they come to him
as dames to an assembly.
Borne on his car with these for his attendants, the god speeds
forth, the universe's monarch.

Travelling on the paths of air's mid-region, no single day
　　doth he take rest or slumber.
Holy and earliest-born, friend of the waters, where did he
　　spring and from what region came he?

Germ of the world, the deities' vital spirit, this god moves
　　ever as his will inclines him.
His voice is heard, his shape is ever viewless. Let us adore
　　this Wind with our oblation.

From the *Rig-Veda*
Translated from the Sanskrit by F. Max Muller

The Song of the Creatures

　Here begin the Lauds of the Creatures which the Blessed
Francis made to the praise and honour of God what time he lay
sick at San Damiano.

　Most high, almighty, and good Lord, Thine be the praise
and glory, the honour and every blessing! To Thee alone,
most High, are they due; and no man is worthy to name Thee.

　Praise to Thee, Lord, with all Thy creatures; and above
all to Brother Sun, who makes the day that lightens us.
Fair he is, and shineth with a great splendour. Most high,
he bears the mark of Thee.

　Praise to Thee, Lord, for Sister Moon, and for the Stars.
In the heavens hast Thou framed them, clear and precious and fair.

　Praise to Thee, Lord, for Brother Wind, for the air and
the cloud, for calm and all weather by which Thou givest
sustenance to Thy creatures.

Praise to Thee, Lord, for Sister Water. Very useful is she, and humble, and precious, and chaste.

Praise to Thee, Lord, for Brother Fire, by whom the night is lightened. Lovely is he and blithe, and lusty and strong.

Praise to Thee, Lord, for our sister, Mother Earth, who upholdeth and careth for us, who brings forth the divers fruit, the painted flowers and the grass.

Praise to Thee, Lord, for those who forgive for love of Thee, and bear weakness and tribulations. Blessed are they who endure in peace, for by Thee, most High, shall they be crowned.

Praise to Thee, Lord, for our Sister, the Death of the Body. From her no man living may escape. Woe unto them that die in mortal sin! Blessed are they who find themselves in Thy most holy will; for the second death cannot harm them.

Praise and bless the Lord, and give Him thanks, and serve Him with great humility.

St Francis of Assisi
Translated from the Italian by Anne MacDowell

From The Book of Hours

I find you in all those things
that make me feel good and brotherly.
You sun yourself as a seed in the small;
you enter the great in your greatness.

It is the wondrous play of the powers,
that they pass through things so serviceably,
they grow in the roots, vanish into the trunk;
at the top – like a resurrection.

RAINER MARIA RILKE
Translated from the German by J. M. Cohen

Now Is Wele

Now is wele and all thing aright
And Crist is come as a trew knight,
For our broder is king of might,
    The fend to fleme* and all his.
Thus the feend is put to flight,
    And all his boost† abated is.

Sithen it is wele, wele we do,
For there is none but one of two,
Heven to gete or heven forgo;
    Oder mene none there is.
I counsaill you, sin it is so,
    That ye wele do to win you bliss.

Now is wele and all is wele,
   And right wele, so have I bliss;
And sithen all thing is so wele,
   I rede‡ we do no more amiss.

ANONYMOUS

* *fleme*: banish
† *boost*: boast
‡ *rede*: advise

Since Nature's Workes be Good

Since Nature's workes be good, and death doth serve
As Nature's worke, why should we feare to die?
Since feare is vaine but when it may preserve,
Why should we feare that which we cannot flie?
Feare is more paine than is the paine it feares,
Disarming humane mindes of native might;
While each conceit an ougly figure beares,
Which were not evill, well view'd in reason's light.
Our only eyes, which dimm'd with passions be,
And scarce discerne the dawne of comming day,
Let them be clear'd, and now begin to see
Our life is but a step in dustie way:
Then let us hold the blisse of peacefull minde,
Since this we feele, great losse we cannot finde.

SIR PHILIP SIDNEY

Our Wars Are Wars of Life

Our wars are wars of life, and wounds of love,
With intellectual spears, and long winged arrows of thought:
Mutual in one anothers love and wrath all renewing
We live as One Man; for contracting our infinite senses
We behold multitude; or expanding: we behold as one,
As One Man all the Universal Family; and that One Man
We call Jesus the Christ: and he in us, and we in him,
Live in perfect harmony in Eden the land of life,
Giving, receiving, and forgiving each others trespasses.
He is the Good shepherd, he is the Lord and master:
He is the Shepherd of Albion, he is all in all,
In Eden: in the garden of God: and in heavenly Jerusalem.

WILLIAM BLAKE
From *Jerusalem* (Chapter 2, Plate 34, lines 14–25)

From Samson Agonistes

All is best, though we oft doubt,
What th'unsearchable dispose
Of highest wisdom brings about,
And ever best found in the close.
Oft he seems to hide his face,
But unexpectedly returns
And to his faithful Champion hath in place
Bore witness gloriously; whence *Gaza* mourns
And all that band them to resist
His uncontroulable intent;
His servants he with new acquist
Of true experience from this great event
With peace and consolation hath dismist,
And calm of mind all passion spent.

JOHN MILTON

Grief is Vain

Thou hast grieved over them for whom grief is unmeet,
though thou speakest words of understanding. The learned
grieve not for them whose lives are fled nor for them
whose lives are not fled.
Never have I not been, never hast thou and never have
these princes of men not been; and never shall time yet
come when we shall not all be.
As the body's tenant goes through childhood and manhood
and old age in this body, so does it pass to other bodies;
the wise man is not confounded therein.
It is the touchings of the senses' instruments, O Kunti's
son, that beget cold and heat, pleasure and pain; it is
they that come and go, that abide not; bear with them, O
thou of Bharata's race.
Verily the man whom these disturb not, indifferent alike to
pain and to pleasure, and wise, is meet for immortality, O
chief of men.
Of what is not there cannot be being; of what is there
cannot be aught but being. The bounds of these twain have
been beheld by them that behold the Verity.
But know that That which pervades this universe is
imperishable; there is none can make to perish that
changeless being.

Bhagavadgita
Lesson The Second, verses 11–17; translated from the Sanskrit by F. Max
Muller

Rebirth of the Corn

GOD: Now night grows drunk,
yet you stand apart from the feasting.
Come, slaughter yourself, put on your garment of gold!

MAN: Downstream goes my God
bearing drops of emerald water,
and the feather-leaved cypress,
the green turquoise serpent,
has given me his blessing.
Let me quench my thirst so that I do not die.
I am the tender corn shoot.
Emerald is my heart. I shall see the gold water.

GOD: My life shall revive
and the young man grow strong.
He who gives the war-cry has been born.

MAN: My Corn-Cob God lifts up his eyes.
Why should I fear?
I am the tender corn shoot.

GOD: From the mountains I come to see you, I, your God.
My life shall revive
and the young man grow strong.
He who gives the war-cry has been born.

ANONYMOUS NAHUATL POEM
Translated from a Spanish version by Irene Nicholson

From Ecclesiastes

Remember now thy Creator in the days of thy youth, while
the evil days come not, nor the years draw nigh, when thou
shalt say, I have no pleasure in them;

While the sun, or the light, or the moon, or the stars,
be not darkened, nor the clouds return after the rain:

In the day when the keepers of the house shall tremble,
and the strong men shall bow themselves, and the grinders
cease because they are few, and those that look out of the
windows be darkened,

And the doors shall be shut in the streets, when the sound
of the grinding is low, and he shall rise up at the voice of
the bird, and all the daughters of musick shall be brought low;

Also when they shall be afraid of that which is high, and
fears shall be in the way, and the almond tree shall flourish,
and the grasshopper shall be a burden, and desire shall fail:
because man goeth to his long home, and the mourners go about
the streets:

Or ever the silver cord be loosed, or the golden bowl be
broken, or the pitcher be broken at the fountain, or the wheel
broken at the cistern.

Then shall the dust return to the earth as it was: and
the spirit shall return unto God who gave it.

Chapter 12. 1–7

The Tenth Duino Elegy

May I, when at the end of this cruel insight,
sing jubilation and praise to assenting angels.
May not one of the firm-hammered keys of my heart
fail to evoke response by touching on slack, uncertain
or bursting strings. May my streaming face
lend me more radiance; may inconspicuous weeping
blossom. O nights of grief, how dear you will be to me then.
Why did I not receive you, inconsolable sisters,
more submissively kneeling, did not surrender myself more freely
into your free-flowing hair? We, the wasters of sorrows.
How we gaze ahead of them, out into sad permanence,
to see if perhaps they might come to an end. But they are
our foliage lasting through winter, our dark evergreen,
one of the inner year's seasons – not only
season – are place, and settlement, camp, soil, and dwelling.

Strange, alas, are the streets of the City of Suffering
where, in the sham silence of sound drowned by sound,
there swaggers, the cast poured forth from the mould of emptiness,
blatant, the gilded noise, the monument bursting apart.
O how an angel would tread underfoot without trace their market
        of consolation
adjoined by the church which they bought ready-made:
clean, disillusioned and closed as a post-office is on a Sunday.
But outside there is always a ripple along the fringe of the fair.
Swings of freedom! Divers and jugglers of zeal!
And the shooting-range figures of prettified happiness,
targets jerking and tinnily clinking whenever
hit by some better marksman. From cheers to chance
he goes staggering on, as booths serving every kind of curiosity
solicit attention, bawl, and beat drums. But there is, in particular,
for adults, the breeding of money on view, anatomical,
not for amusement only: the sex part of money,
the whole of it, all the act – instructive, ensuring
fertility . . .
        Oh, but quite close, just beyond it,
behind the last hoarding plastered with posters for 'Deathless',
the bitter beer that seems sweet to those who consume it

when, as they drink, they continually chew fresh distractions,
just at the back of the hoarding, there, just behind, it is *real*:
children at play, and lovers holding each other, aside,
gravely, in shabby grass, and dogs obeying their instincts.
The youth is drawn farther away; it may be that he loves
a youthful Lament . . . Behind her, he walks into meadows. She says:
'Far away. We are living out there . . .'
                                        Where? And he follows.
He is touched by her bearing. Her shoulder, her neck – perhaps
she is of noble descent. But he leaves her, turns back,
faces round, and waves . . . What does it avail? She is a Lament.

Only the youthful dead, in their first condition
of timeless serenity, of becoming weaned,
follow her lovingly. Girls
she waits for, befriends them. Shows them gently
what she wears on her person. The pearls of suffering,
the finely woven veils of endurance. – Youths
she walks with in silence.

But, where they live, in the valley, one of the older
Laments responds to the youth when he asks. 'We were once,'
she says, 'a great family, we, the Laments. Our fathers
worked the mines in those towering mountains; at times, among
        humans,
you find a piece of polished primeval suffering
or, from an ancient volcano, drossy petrified wrath.
Yes, that had its origin there. We were rich once.'

And leading him lightly through the spacious landscape of Laments,
she shows him the columns of temples, the ruins
of strongholds from which, in the past, the sovereign princes
of the House of Lament had wisely governed the land.
Shows him the tall tear-trees, the fields of flowering sadness
(known to the living only as tender foliage);
shows him the grazing creatures of grief – and at times
a startled bird, in its level flight through their lifted gaze,
traces the long-drawn trail of its lonely cry.

In the evening she leads him up to the graves of the eldest
of the House of Lament, the sibyls and seers.
But, night drawing near, they move more softly, and soon,
moon-like, there rises before them, guarding all things,
the sepulchral monument. Brother to that by the Nile,
the lofty Sphinx – the reticent chamber's face.
And they marvel at the regal head which, for ever,
has silently poised human vision
upon the scale of the stars.

His glance does not grasp it, dizzy
with early death. But her gaze
starts an owl from behind the rim of the *pshent.*[*]
Brushing in slowly descending flight
along the cheek with the richest curve,
it softly traces across the new
death-given hearing, over an open
double page, the indescribable outline.

And, higher, the stars. New ones. Stars of the land of suffering.
The Lament slowly names them: 'There,
see: the Horseman, the Staff, and they call the more crowded
constellation the Garland of Fruit. Then, nearer the Pole:
Cradle, Way, The Burning Book, Doll, and Window.
But in the southern sky, pure as in the palm
of a blessed hand, the translucid M
which signifies Mothers . . .'

But he, the dead youth, must go on, and the older Lament
silently takes him as far as the gorge
where it gleams in the moonlight:
the Source of Joy. With reverence
she names it, and says: 'Among humans,
it is a carrying stream.'

They stand at the foot of the mountains.
And there she embraces him, weeping.

Alone, he climbs to the Hills of Primeval Suffering.
And in soundless fate not even his steps make a sound.

But if they, the endlessly dead, evoked a symbol to us,
look, they might point to the catkins hanging from bare
hazels, or else bring to mind
the rain that falls on dark earth in the spring.

And we, who think of *ascending*
happiness, would experience
the feeling which almost startles
when what is happy *falls*.

RAINER MARIA RILKE
Translated from the German by Ruth Speirs
* *pshent*: the Pharaonic crown symbolizing the unity of Upper and Lower Egypt

Resurgam

From depth to height, from height to loftier height,
The climber sets his foot and sets his face,
Tracks lingering sunbeams to their halting-place,
And counts the last pulsations of the light.
Strenuous thro' day and unsurprised by night
He runs a race with Time and wins the race,
Emptied and stripped of all save only Grace,
Will, Love, a threefold panoply of might.
Darkness descends for light he toiled to seek:
He stumbles on the darkened mountain-head,
Left breathless in the unbreathable thin air,
Made freeman of the living and the dead: –
He wots not he has topped the topmost peak,
But the returning sun will find him there.

CHRISTINA ROSSETTI

Many Births

Many births of me and thee have passed, O Arjuna. I
know them all; but thou knowest them not, O affrighter
of the foe.
Though birthless and unchanging of essence, and though
lord of born beings, yet in my sway over the Nature that
is mine own I come into birth by my own magic.
For whensoever the law fails and lawlessness uprises, O
thou of Bharata's race, then do I bring myself to bodied
birth.
To guard the righteous, to destroy evildoers, to establish
the law, I come into birth age after age.
He who knows in verity my divine birth and works comes
not again to birth when he has left the body; he comes
to me, O Arjuna.
Many, freed from passion, fear, and wrath, instinct with
me, making their home in me, and cleansed by the mortifications
of knowledge, have come into my Being.
With them that seek me I deal in like measure.

Bhagavadgita
Lesson The Fourth, verses 5–11; translated from the Sanskrit by F. Max Muller

Hamlet

The tumult stills. I stand upon the stage
Against a door-post, dimly reckoning
From traces of a distantly heard echo
What my unfinished lifetime may yet bring.

The black of night pours from these opera glasses
That in their thousands train their sights on me:
But Abba, Father, if it be your will,
Remove this chalice in your clemency.

Unswervingly your purpose holds my love,
This rôle you've set I am content to play;
But now a different drama takes the scene:
Spare me this once the treading of your way.

And yet the order of the acts is planned,
The way's end destinate and unconcealed.
Alone. Now is the time of Pharisees.
To live is not like walking through a field.

BORIS PASTERNAK
Translated from the Russian by Henry Kamen

What is This Life?

What is this LIFE of ours? a *Bubble* weake
  That swelleth on the Water in the Raine,
  To die as soone as thou canst see it plaine,
Bursting asunder at the slightest Freake.
What is this LIFE of ours? a tickle *Tricke*
  That fooles us with a shadow of true gaine;
  A *Dreame*, whose puissance doth not long remaine –
Unglew thy Liddes: his vertues vanish quicke!
What is this life of ours? a whirling *Eddy*
Of gray Light mocking in the Ayre unsteady,
  Swifter to passe than Lightning's murd'rous Stroak.
Henceforth ye shall forsake th' *Idaea* of Bliss
That standeth faste, and knowe your State is this –
  A Puffe, a Tricke, a Dreame, a Dunghill Smoak!

JEAN-BAPTISTE CHASSIGNET
Translated from the French by Kenneth S. Kitchin

Unanswered Question

What is the end of all things – life or grave?
Is it the upholding, or the whelming, wave?
So many tangled tracks whose distant goal
Is what? The cradle holds – fate or man's soul?
Are we below, in blest or wretched state,
Predestined kings, or pawns foredoomed of fate?
Didst Thou, oh God, say, Lord Almighty, say,
Create man but to tread his destined way?
Say, does the crib the cross already hold?
These silken nests, touched by cool dawn with gold,
Where amid flowers budding plumes expand,
Were they for small fowls or for fowlers planned?

VICTOR HUGO
Translated from the French by R. J. P. Hewison

Upon the Image of Death

Before my face the picture hangs,
    That daily should put me in mind
Of those cold qualms and bitter pangs,
    That shortly I am like to find:
        But yet, alas, full little I
        Do think hereon that I must die.

I often look upon a face
    Most ugly, grisly, bare, and thin;
I often view the hollow place,
    Where eyes and nose had sometimes been;
        I see the bones across that lie,
        Yet little think that I must die.

I read the label underneath,
   That telleth me whereto I must;
I see the sentence eke that saith
   'Remember, man, that thou art dust!'
      But yet, alas, but seldom I
      Do think indeed that I must die.

Continually at my bed's head
   A hearse doth hang, which doth me tell,
That I ere morning may be dead,
   Though now I feel myself full well:
      But yet, alas, for all this, I
      Have little mind that I must die.

The gown which I do use to wear,
   The knife wherewith I cut my meat,
And eke that old and ancient chair
   Which is my only usual seat;
      All these do tell me I must die,
      And yet my life amend not I.

My ancestors are turned to clay,
   And many of my mates are gone;
My youngers daily drop away,
   And can I think to 'scape alone?
      No, no, I know that I must die,
      And yet my life amend not I.

Not Solomon, for all his wit,
   Nor Samson, though he were so strong,
No king nor person ever yet
   Could 'scape, but death laid him along:
      Wherefore I know that I must die,
      And yet my life amend not I.

Though all the East did quake to hear
  Of Alexander's dreadful name,
And all the West did likewise fear
  To hear of Julius Caesar's fame,
    Yet both by death in dust now lie.
    Who then can 'scape but he must die?

If none can 'scape death's dreadful dart,
  If rich and poor his beck obey,
If strong, if wise, if all do smart,
  Then I to 'scape shall have no way.
    Oh! grant me grace, O God, that I
    My life may mend, sith I must die.

ROBERT SOUTHWELL

Whispers of Heavenly Death

Darest thou now O soul,
Walk out with me toward the unknown region,
Where neither ground is for the feet nor any path to follow?

No map there, nor guide,
Nor voice sounding, nor touch of human hand,
Nor face with blooming flesh, nor lips, nor eyes, are in that land.

I know it not O soul,
Nor dost thou, all is a blank before us,
All waits undream'd of in that region, that inaccessible land.

Till when the ties loosen,
All but the ties eternal, Time and Space,
Nor darkness, gravitation, sense, nor any bounds bounding us.

224

Then we burst forth, we float,
In Time and Space O soul, prepared for them,
Equal, equipt at last, (O joy! O fruit of all!) them to fulfil O soul.

Whispers of heavenly death murmur'd I hear,
Labial gossip of night, sibilant chorals,
Footsteps gently ascending, mystical breezes wafted soft and low,
Ripples of unseen rivers, tides of a current flowing, forever flowing,
(Or is it the plashing of tears? the measureless waters of human
        tears?)

I see, just see skyward, great cloud-masses,
Mournfully slowly they roll, silently swelling and mixing,
With at times a half-dimm'd sadden'd far-off star,
Appearing and disappearing.

(Some parturition rather, some solemn immortal birth;
On the frontiers to eyes impenetrable,
Some soul is passing over.)

WALT WHITMAN

225

The Dying Man

The dying man saw
mysterious gestures, forgotten faces
pass before his eyes,
birds of another country once his own
(but in a foreign sky).

Through the open window came the earthy
colour of the storm.
He heard the rustling of the olives
far-off, in his distant childhood,
wind-tossed now.

The air crackled with sharp reports.

He saw the fields, the sun,
the south, the years, the distance.

An opaque sky stretched
over a foreign land.

         In a slow voice
he assembled all that was scattered,
collected features and names,
the heat of all those hands
and shining days,
into a single sigh,
huge and powerful
as life.

Finally rain broke the dark siege.
Memory expanded.

         May song
bear witness for him
that in this struggle he won self-completion.

José Angel Valente
Translated from the Spanish by J. M. Cohen

A Death

'His face shone' she said,
'Three days I had him in my house,
Three days before they took him from his bed,
And never have I felt so close.'

'Always alive he was
A little drawn away from me.
Looks are opaque when living and his face
Seemed hiding something, carefully.'

'But those three days before
They took his body out, I used to go
And talk to him. That shining from him bore
No secrets. Living, he never looked or answered so.'

Sceptic I listened, then
Noted what peace she seemed to have,
How tenderly she put flowers on his grave
But not as if he might return again
Or shine or seem quite close:
Rather to please us were the flowers she gave.

ELIZABETH JENNINGS

Unity of Spirit

When the rose is dead and the garden ravaged, where shall
    we find the perfume of the rose? In rose-water.
Inasmuch as God comes not into sight, the prophets are
    His vicars.
Do not mistake me! 'Tis wrong to think that the vicar
    and He Whom the vicar represents are two.
To the form-worshipper they are two; when you have escaped
    from consciousness of form, they are One.

Whilst you regard the form, you are seeing double: look,
 not at the eyes, but at the light which flows from them.
You cannot distinguish the lights of ten lamps burning together,
 so long as your face is set towards this light alone.
In things spiritual there is no partition, no number, no
 individuals.
How sweet is the oneness of the Friend with His friends!
 Catch the spirit and clasp it to your bosom.
Mortify rebellious form till it wastes away: unearth the
 treasure of Unity!

Simple were we and all one essence: we were knotless and
 pure as water.
When that goodly Light took shape, it became many, like
 shadows cast by a battlement.
Demolish the dark battlement, and all difference will vanish
 from amidst this multitude.

From the *Mathnawī* of RŪMĪ
Translated from the Persian by R. A. Nicholson

I Must Launch Out my Boat

I must launch out my boat. The languid hours
pass by on the shore – Alas for me!
 The spring has done its flowering and taken leave.
And now with the burden of faded futile flowers I
wait and linger.
 The waves have become clamorous, and upon the bank
in the shady lane the yellow leaves flutter and fall.
 What emptiness do you gaze upon! Do you not feel
a thrill passing through the air with the notes of
the far-away song floating from the other shore?

RABINDRANATH TAGORE

The Ladder of Paradise

Within the crystal's ever-circling sphere –
    Named after its bright regent, him whose reign
    Made wickedness to die and disappear, –
Coloured like gold which flashes back again
    The sun, I saw a ladder stand, that seemed
    So high that the eye followed it in vain.
Moreover on the rungs descending gleamed
    So many splendours that each several star
    From heaven, methought, collected thither, streamed.
As rooks, after their natural habit, fare
    Forth all together at beginning day
    To warm their feathers chilled by the night air;
Then some, without returning, wing away,
    Some to the boughs they have their nests among
    Return, and others circling make a stay;
Such a behaviour had that sparkling throng,
    It seemed to me, coming in bands abreast,
    Soon as they lighted on a certain rung.
And that one which most near to us came to rest
    Became so bright that I said in my thought:
    'I see the love to me thou signallest.'

DANTE ALIGHIERI
Paradiso, xxi. 25–45. Translated from the Italian by Laurence Binyon

Love as the Ruler of the Universe

The whole world is a market-place for Love,
For naught that is, from Love remains remote.
The Eternal Wisdom made all things in Love:
On Love they all depend, to Love all turn.
The earth, the heavens, the sun, the moon, the stars,
The Centre of their orbit find in Love.
By Love are all bewildered, stupefied,

Intoxicated by the Wine of Love.
From each a mystic silence Love demands.
What do all seek so earnestly? 'Tis Love.
What do they whisper to each other? Love.
Love is the subject of their inmost thoughts.
In Love no longer 'thou' and 'I' exist,
For Self has passed away in the Beloved.
Now will I draw aside the veil from Love,
And in the temple of mine inmost soul,
Behold the Friend, Incomparable Love.
He who would know the secret of both worlds,
Will find the secret of them both, is Love.

'ATTĀR
From the *Jawhar Al-Dhāt*
Translated from the Persian by Margaret Smith

Chorus of the Unborn

We the unborn
The yearning has begun to plague us
The shores of blood broaden to receive us
Like dew we sink into love
But still the shadows of time lie like questions
Over our secret.

You who love,
You who yearn,
Listen, you who are sick with parting:
We are those who begin to live in your glances,
In your hands which are searching the blue air –
We are those who smell of morning.
Already your breath is inhaling us,
Drawing us down into your sleep

230

Into the dreams which are our earth
Where night, our black nurse,
Lets us grow
Until we mirror ourselves in your eyes
Until we speak into your ear.

We are caught
Like butterflies by the sentries of your yearning –
Like birdsong sold to earth –
We who smell of morning,
We future lights for your sorrow.

NELLY SACHS
Translated from the German by Ruth and Matthew Mead

Cobwebs

It is a land with neither night nor day,
Nor heat nor cold, nor any wind nor rain,
Nor hills nor valleys: but one even plain
Stretches through long unbroken miles away,
While through the sluggish air a twilight grey
Broodeth: no moons or seasons wax and wane,
No ebb and flow are there along the main,
No bud-time, no leaf-falling, there for aye: –
No ripple on the sea, no shifting sand,
No beat of wings to stir the stagnant space:
No pulse of life through all the loveless land
And loveless sea; no trace of days before,
No guarded home, no toil-won resting-place,
No future hope, no fear for evermore.

CHRISTINA ROSSETTI

From a Tablet Found in an Orphic Tomb

To him who, purified, would break this vicious round
And breathe once more the air of heaven – greeting!
There in the courts of Hades wilt thou find
Leftward a beckoning cypress, tall and bright,
From out whose root doth flow the water of Oblivion.
Approach it not: guard thou thy thirst awhile.
For on the other hand – and further – wells
From bottomless pool the limpid stream of Memory,
Cool, full of refreshment. To its guardians cry thus:
'I am the child of earth and starry sky:
Know that I too am heavenly – but parched!
I perish: give then and quickly that clear draught
Of ice-cold Memory!' And from that fountainhead divine
Straightway they'll give thee drink; quaffing the which
Thou with the other heroes eternally shalt rule.

Translated from the Greek; translator unknown

From The Brihadāraṇyaka Upanishad

This earth is the honey (madhu, the effect) of all beings, and all beings
are the honey (madhu, the effect) of this earth. Likewise this bright,
immortal person in this earth, and that bright immortal person
incorporated in the body (both are madhu). He indeed is the same as
that Self, that Immortal, that Brahman, that All.

This water is the honey of all beings, and all beings are the honey of this
water. Likewise this bright, immortal person in this water, and that
bright, immortal person, existing as seed in the body (both are madhu).
He indeed is the same as that Self, that Immortal, that Brahman, that
All.

This fire is the honey of all beings, and all beings are the honey of this fire. Likewise this bright, immortal person in this fire, and that bright, immortal person, existing as speech in the body (both are madhu). He indeed is the same as that Self, that Immortal, that Brahman, that All.

This air is the honey of all beings, and all beings are the honey of this air. Likewise this bright, immortal person in this air, and that bright, immortal person existing as breath in the body (both are madhu). He indeed is the same as that Self, that Immortal, that Brahman, that All.

This sun is the honey of all beings, and all beings are the honey of this sun. Likewise this bright, immortal person in this sun, and that bright, immortal person existing as the eye in the body (both are madhu). He indeed is the same as that Self, that Immortal, that Brahman, that All.

This space (diśah, the quarters) is the honey of all beings, and all beings are the honey of this space. Likewise this bright, immortal person in this space, and that bright, immortal person existing as the ear in the body (both are madhu). He indeed is the same as that Self, that Immortal, that Brahman, that All.

This moon is the honey of all beings, and all beings are the honey of this moon. Likewise this bright, immortal person in this moon, and that bright, immortal person existing as mind in the body (both are madhu). He indeed is the same as that Self, that Immortal, that Brahman, that All.

Translated from the Sanskrit by F. Max Muller

Neither Samsara* nor Nirvana†

Here there is no beginning, no middle, no end,
Neither samsara nor nirvana.
In this state of highest bliss
There is neither self nor other.

Whatever you see, that is it,
In front, behind, in all the ten directions.
Even today let your master make an end of delusion!
There is no need to ask of anyone else.

The faculties of sense subside,
And the notion of self is destroyed.
O friend, such is the Body Innate.
Ask for it clearly of your master.

Where thought is held and breath passes hence,
That is the highest bliss.
Elsewhere one goes nowhere.

From *Saraha's Treasury of Songs*
Translated from the Tibetan by D. Snellgrove

* *Samsara*: the relative world of illusion
† *Nirvana*: the bliss of non-being

Meru

Civilisation is hooped together, brought
Under a rule, under the semblance of peace
By manifold illusion; but man's life is thought,
And he, despite his terror, cannot cease
Ravening through century after century,
Ravening, raging, and uprooting that he may come
Into the desolation of reality:
Egypt and Greece, good-bye, and good-bye, Rome!
Hermits upon Mount Meru or Everest,

Caverned in night under the drifted snow,
Or where that snow and winter's dreadful blast
Beat down upon their naked bodies, know
That day brings round the night, that before dawn
His glory and his monuments are gone.

W. B. YEATS

O Light Eternal

O Light Eternal, who in thyself alone
   Dwell'st and thyself know'st, and self-understood,
   Self-understanding, smilest on thine own!
That circle which, as I conceived it, glowed
   Within thee like reflection of a flame,
   Being by mine eyes a little longer wooed,
Deep in itself, with colour still the same,
   Seemed with our human effigy to fill,
   Wherefore absorbed in it my sight became.
As the geometer who bends all his will
   To measure the circle, and howsoe'er he try
   Fails, for the principle escapes him still,
Such at this mystery new-disclosed was I,
   Fain to understand how the image doth alight
   Upon the circle, and with its form comply.
But these my wings were fledged not for that flight,
   Save that my mind a sudden glory assailed
   And its wish came revealed to it in that light.
To the high imagination force now failed;
   But like to a wheel whose circling nothing jars
   Already on my desire and will prevailed
The Love that moves the sun and the other stars.

DANTE ALIGHIERI
Paradiso, xxxiii. 124–45. Translated from the Italian by Laurence Binyon

The Ultimate Release

Know the taste of this flavour which consists in absence of knowledge.
Those who recite commentaries do not know how to cleanse the world.

Listen, my son; this taste cannot be told by its various parts.
For it is free from conceits, a state of perfect bliss, in which existence
    has its origin.

It is the very last segment that remains of the creation of illusion,
Where intellect is destroyed, where mind dies and self-centredness is
    lost.
Why encumber yourself there with meditation?

A thing appears in the world and then goes to destruction.
If it has no true existence, how may it appear again?
If it is free from both manifestation and destruction, what then arises?
Stay! Your master has spoken.

From *Saraha's Treasury of Songs*
Translated from the Tibetan by D. Snellgrove

From The Cherubic Wanderer

Sin is no more than this: that a man turns his head
away from God, and looks towards death instead.

ANGELUS SILESIUS
Translated from the German by J. M. Cohen

Faust's Assumption

THE SINGLE PENITENT (formerly named Gretchen):
>By choirs of noble souls surrounded
>This new one scarcely feels his soul,
>Can scarcely sense this life unbounded,
>Yet fills at once his heavenly role.
>See how he sheds the earthly leaven,
>Tears off each shroud of old untruth,
>And from apparel woven in heaven
>Shines forth his pristine power of youth!
>Mary, grant me to instruct him,
>Dazzled as yet by this new day.

MATER GLORIOSA:
>Come then! To higher spheres conduct him!
>Divining *you*, he knows the way.

DOCTOR MARIANUS (bowing in adoration):
>All you tender penitents,
>Gaze on her who saves you –
>Thus you change your lineaments
>And salvation laves you.
>To her feet each virtue crawl,
>Let her will transcend us;
>Virgin, Mother, Queen of All,
>Goddess, still befriend us!

CHORUS MYSTICUS:
>All that is past of us
>Was but reflected;
>All that was lost in us
>Here is corrected;
>All indescribables
>Here we descry;
>Eternal Womanhead
>Leads us on high.

J. W. VON GOETHE
From *Faust*. Translated from the German by Louis MacNeice

ENVOI
From The Cherubic Wanderer

Friend, you have read enough. If you desire still more,
Then be the poem yourself, and all that it stands for.

ANGELUS SILESIUS
Translated from the German by J. M. Cohen

Index of Authors

ABU-AL-'ALĀ' AL-MA'ARRI (973–1057)
Blind Arabic poet of Baghdad. 16,
136

AL-HALLAJ, HUSEIN IBN MANSUR
(857–922) Sufi writer and
occasional poet of Baghdad. He was
executed for his heretical teachings.
172

ANDERSON, WILLIAM (b. 1935)
English poet and writer on Dante
and the Gothic. 64, 69

ANGELUS SILESIUS (1624–77) German
composer of gnomic verses. 98,
105, 159, 202, 204, 236, 238

'ATTĀR, FARID UD-DĪN
(1119–?1229) Persian Sufi poet,
famous for his allegory *The
Parliament of the Birds*. 175, 191,
229

BATE, JOHN (b. 1919) English poet
and librarian, living in Edinburgh.
158

BHARTRHARI Hindu poet who wrote
in Sanskrit in the first half of the
7th century AD. 106

BLAKE, WILLIAM (1757–1827) English
poet and engraver. 65, 86, 133,
138, 140, 181, 193, 212

BLOK, ALEXANDER (1880–1921)
Russian poet. 19

BRIDGES, ROBERT SEYMOUR
(1844–1930) English poet. 81, 132

BUONARROTI, MICHELANGELO
(1475–1564) Painter, sculptor,
architect and poet. 33, 40

CAMPANELLA, TOMASO (1568–1630)
Italian friar, who was imprisoned
for his radical religious views. 25,
34

CAMPION, THOMAS (1567–1620)
English poet and musician. 74

CARDENAL, ERNESTO (b. 1925)
Nicaraguan priest and poet of
revolutionary views. 6

CEPPÈDE, JEAN DE LA (1550–1622)
French Baroque poet. 89

CHASSIGNET, JEAN-BAPTISTE
(1570–1635) French Baroque poet.
221

CORNISH, WILLIAM (14?–1523)
English poet. 84

COWPER, WILLIAM (1731–1800)
English poet. 59, 74, 83

CRASHAW, RICHARD (1613?–1649)
English Meraphysical poet.

CUZA MALÉ, BELKIS (b. 1942) Cuban
poet living in the United States.
95, 149

DANIEL, SAMUEL (1562–1619) English
poet and dramatist. 12

DANTE ALIGHIERI (1265–1321) Italian
poet of *La Divina Commedia*. 3, 15,
203, 229, 235

DICKINSON, EMILY (1830–86)
American poet. 60, 92, 98, 153,
170

DIEGO, ELISEO (6. 1920) Coban poet.
76

DONNE, JOHN (1572–1631) English
Metaphysical poet and Dean of St
Paul's. 35, 39, 41, 46, 107, 113

DROSTE-HÜLSHOFF, ANNETTE VON
(1797–1848) German poet. 60

DYER, SIR EDWARD (1543–1607)
English poet. 173

EBERHART, RICHARD (b. 1904)
American poet. 53

EMRE, YUNUS (?–1321) Turkish poet.
177

239

Acknowledgements

The editor and publishers gratefully acknowledge permission to use the following copyright poems in this anthology:

Lines from Dante, 'Encounter in Hell' (p. 3), 'The Hell of the Winds' (p. 15), 'Ascent into Paradise' (p. 203), 'The Ladder of Paradise' (p. 229), and 'O Light Eternal' (p. 235). From *The Divine Comedy*, translated by Laurence Binyon. Reprinted by permission of Mrs Nicolete Gray and The Society of Authors on behalf of the Laurence Binyon Estate.

Lines from Goethe, 'Faust's Confession' (p. 5) and 'Faust's Assumption' (p. 237). Reprinted by permission of Faber and Faber Ltd from *Goethe's Faust* translated by Louis MacNeice.

'Bill of Sale' (p. 16) and 'The Comet' (p. 136). Reprinted by permission of Penguin Books Ltd from *Birds Through a Ceiling of Alabaster*, transl. Abdullah al-Udhari and George Wightman (Penguin Classics 1975), pp. 102,104. Copyright © G.B.H. Wightman and A.Y. al-Udhari, 1975.

'The Muck Farmer' (p. 16) and 'Green Categories' (p. 52). Reprinted by permission of Granada Publishing Limited from *Poetry for Supper* by R.S. Thomas.

'The Puppet' (p. 17). Transl. I.B. Horner. Reprinted by permission of Bruno Cassirer (Publishers) Ltd, Oxford.

'The Eighth Duino Elegy' (p. 19), 'The Mystery' (p. 131), and 'The Tenth Duino Elegy' (p. 216). Translations reprinted by permission of Ruth Speirs.

'A Reminder of the End' (p. 23). Reprinted by permission of The Society of Authors as the literary representative of the Estate of John Masefield. Reprinted with permission of Macmillan Publishing Co., Inc., from *Poems* by John Masefield. Copyright 1912 by Macmillan Publishing Co., Inc., renewed 1940 by John Masefield.

'The Golden Goose Speaks' (p. 24). From Edward Conze (transl.), *The Buddha's Law among the Birds*, Bruno Cassirer (Publishers) Ltd, Oxford.

'The Second Coming' (p. 24), 'The Four Ages of Man' (p. 51), 'The Cold Heaven' (p. 65), and 'Meru' (p. 234). From *Collected Poems of W.B. Yeats*. Reprinted by permission of A.P. Watt Ltd on behalf of Michael and Anne Yeats and Macmillan London Limited. Reprinted with permission of Macmillan Publishing Co., Inc., from *Collected Poems* by William Butler Yeats. 'The Second Coming', copyright 1924 by Macmillan Publishing Co., Inc., renewed 1952 by Bertha Georgie Yeats; 'The Four Ages of Man' and 'Meru', copyright 1934 by Macmillan Publishing Co., Inc., renewed 1962 by Bertha Georgie Yeats; 'The Cold Heaven', copyright 1912 by Macmillan Publishing Co., Inc., renewed 1940 by Bertha Georgie Yeats.

'If Thy Soul is a Stranger to Thee' (p. 32), 'Neither Manifest Nor Hidden' (p. 159), and 'The Spirit of the Quest' (p. 187). From Rabindranath Tagore (transl.), *A Hundred Poems of Kabir*, by permission of Macmillan, London and Basingstoke. From Rabindranath Tagore: *One Hundred Poems of Kabir* (New York, Macmillan, 1950). Reprinted with permission of Macmillan Publishing Co., Inc.

'To a Friend with a Religious Vocation' (p. 42), 'At a Mass' (p. 93), 'Teresa of Avila' (p. 96), and 'A Death' (p. 227). Elizabeth Jennings, from *Penguin Poets 1*. Reprinted by permission of David Higham Associates Limited.

'De Profundis' (p. 43), 'Kyrie' (p. 48), and 'Ex Nihilo' (p. 115). From David Gascoyne's *Collected Poems*, © Oxford University Press 1965. Reprinted by permission of Oxford University Press.

243

244

of Shiraz, transl. Peter Avery and John Heath-Stubbs. Reprinted by permission of John Murray (Publishers) Ltd.

'Nothing There but Faith' (p. 92). Reprinted by permission of Faber and Faber Ltd from *The Collected Poems of Edwin Muir*. From *Collected Poems by Edwin Muir*. Copyright © 1960 by Willa Muir. Reprinted by permission of Oxford University Press, Inc.

'Magic Strings' (p. 94). Reprinted by permission of Penguin Books Ltd from *Poems of the Late T'ang*, transl. A.C. Graham (Penguin Classics 1965), p. 94. Copyright © A.C. Graham, 1965.

'Truth of All Truth' (p. 103) and 'Apologia' (p. 105). From *Mediaeval Latin Lyrics* by Helen Waddell (Penguin Classics 1952), pp. 135, 209. Reprinted by permission of A.P. Watt Ltd on behalf of the Estate of Helen Waddell and Constable and Co. Ltd. Reprinted from *Mediaeval Latin Lyrics*. Translated by Helen Waddell, by permission of W.W. Norton & Company, Inc. All rights reserved, 1977.

'Christ's Bounties' (p. 103). Reprinted by permission of Routledge & Kegan Paul Ltd from *A Celtic Miscellany: Translations from the Celtic Literatures* by Kenneth H. Jackson (Routledge & Kegan Paul Ltd, 1967).

'Blessing' (p. 104). From *That Singing Flesh* by Terence Tiller. Reprinted by permission of the author and Chatto & Windus Ltd.

'Patience' (p. 106). Reprinted by permission of Penguin Books Ltd from *Poems from the Sanskrit*, John Brough (Penguin Classics 1968), p. 71. Copyright © John Brough, 1968.

'Prayer' (p. 116), 'To Give the World for Nothing' (p. 118), and 'Glory to the Lord' (p. 177). From *The Penguin Book of Turkish Verse*, 1978, edited by Nermin Menemencioğlu and Fahir Iz, pp. 125, 129–130. Reprinted by permission of Nermin Menemencioğlu.

Devotion to Avalokiteşvara (p. 123), 'Beyond Thought' (p. 139), 'On Reading the Dhyana Sutra' (p. 145), 'On Trust in his Heart (p. 160), 'Neither Samsara nor Nirvana' (p. 234), and 'The Ultimate Release' (p. 236). From Edward Conze (transl.), *Buddhist Texts*, Bruno Cassirer (Publishers) Ltd, Oxford.

'Lord of the Ring' (p. 125) and 'Rebirth of the Corn' (p. 214). Reprinted by permission of Faber and Faber Ltd from *Firefly in the Night* by Irene Nicholson.

'Mutability' (p. 134). From *Penguin Modern Poets 25*, 1975, p. 76. Reprinted by permission of the author and Anthony Shiel Ltd.

'The Swords of Glass' (p. 143). From *Reading a Medal* by Terence Tiller. Reprinted by permission of the author and Chatto & Windus Ltd.

'The Terraced Valley' (p. 150). From *Collected Poems*, Robert Graves, Cassell, 1965. Reprinted by permission of the author and A.P. Watt Ltd.

'Visionary Moment' (p. 153). From *The Oxford Book of Russian Verse* chosen by Maurice Baring (2nd edition 1948). Reprinted by permission of Oxford University Press.

'Optical Illusion' (p. 155). From *Collected Poems*, Kathleen Raine, Hamish Hamilton, 1956. Reprinted by permission of the author and George Allen & Unwin (Publishers) Ltd.

'The Fountain' (p. 156). Denise Levertov, *The Jacob's Ladder*. Copyright © 1961 by Denise Levertov Goodman. Reprinted by permission of New Directions Publishing Corporation.

'Poem Written Shortly Before Death' (p. 157). From *Poems* by Rabindranath Tagore published by Visva-Bharati, Calcutta 1942, p. 127. Reprinted by permission of Macmillan, London and Basingstoke.

'Rublev's Icon' (p. 158). Reprinted by permission of the author.